BETTY AUTREY

classroom craft activities:

—— featuring ——

50 seasonal ideas

Classroom
Craft
Activities:

——featuring——

50 Seasonal Ideas

Peggy Palmer

Parker Publishing Company, Inc., West Nyack, New York

Library of Congress Cataloging in Publication Data

Palmer, Peggy
   Classroom craft activities.

   Includes index.
   1. Creative activities and seat work. 2. Handicraft.
I. Title.
LB1537.P34   372.5   76-49569
ISBN 0-13-136168-6

Printed in the United States of America

to all God's children

*and in loving appreciation
to my husband Bill
and my children,
Jenni and Billy*

A Word from the Author

Learning can be fun!

This book is packed with entertaining and educational craft activities for elementary school-aged children.

Not only does it contain a wide variety of interesting, creative and educational activities, but it features more than 50 seasonal, decorative and useful gift ideas to suit all your special needs.

The craft activities are designed to lighten your work load and to delight your students, while stimulating their imagination, ingenuity, self-satisfaction, learning and growth.

The book is divided into 12 chapters, each chapter dealing with a specific media or material, allowing you to quickly and confidently select a suitable craft activity.

Visual aids such as photographs, illustrations and patterns have been provided for your further assistance. A list of supplies and materials required precedes the instructions for each activity to further expedite your selection. Helpful "teaching tips" follow the activity directions, providing you with useful suggestions, seasonal change ideas, age adaptations, additional time-saving hints and safety measures.

When an activity is conducted for the first time, it is always a good idea to arrange a classroom demonstration or to have a prepared sample craft on display for children to see. Demonstrating or displaying a completed project while instructions are given helps students to visualize the craft immediately, while also providing a goal for the activity.

Most of the materials required for these activities are inexpensive, and many can be found for free or at a minimum cost.

A "Where To Find It" supply source list is also included as an appendix at the end of the text. Students can bring supplies from home or work in groups and collect materials.

The educational values and benefits of classroom craft activities are inherent. Through participation in an enjoyable activity, each student discards inhibition and self-consciousness. Total concentration is focused on what he or she is doing.

Some inherent values of classroom craft activities are manual dexterity, mental maturation, patience, physical development, coordination, optical skills, perception and imagination.

Evaluating a student's handiwork depends upon many factors. Each project is the result of an individual effort. These efforts depend upon the student's mental and physical age, home environment, attitude, desire and talent.

Classroom craft activities are not contests; they are fun projects with definite educational benefits. Perfection is not a goal. Self-expression, learning and doing are more important.

Classroom Craft Activities: Featuring 50 Seasonal Ideas can help you provide your students with entertaining, inexpensive, all-occasion projects utilizing various media, while challenging them with new and different activities that allow you to achieve educational goals through constructive, creative activities.

Happy Creating!

Peggy Palmer

Acknowledgements

Thanks to the encouragement and knowledgeable assistance of some very special individuals, this book is a reality.

I extend my deepest appreciation to my patient, hard-working husband, Bill, for his labor both behind the camera and in the darkroom, and to my two best helpers, my children Jenni and Billy.

Special thanks to author Vicki Crume for her valuable tips and encouragement. Grateful appreciation to photographer Richard Shepherd, Osceola County librarian Eleanor Gentry, illustrator Ron Grathwol, writer Peggy McLaughlin and the indispensable Dr. William J. Tait. And, to five lovely, dedicated teachers —Judy Davis, Frances Partin, Carmen Visconti, Beverly Partin and Frances Snyder—for their helpful assistance.

Many thanks also to Principal William Ketchersid, the staff and faculty of Central Avenue Elementary School, Kissimmee, Fl. and artist Frances Smith for providing a "testing ground" for many of the activities in this book.

And last, but certainly not least, I want to thank my family and friends for their understanding during my many months of creative hibernation.

P.P.

Table of Contents

chapter one —

Make and Play

Today, too few children know how to entertain themselves. This first chapter lets students create their own fun. They can make these "crafty" toys and play with them at school or at home.

The activities in this fun chapter will help develop students' individuality, ingenuity, imagination and self-confidence. While most of the crafts will probably be carried home, save some for classroom fun on rainy, snowbound or special days.

Educational values in this chapter include manual dexterity, physical coordination, balance, perspective, throwing and catching, spatial relations, patience, design and color coordination.

Soaring Saucer

—aluminum pie pan makes soaring fun!

materials

- 2 alike aluminum pie pans
- black felt-tipped pen (kind that writes on anything)
- stapler
- felt scraps (optional)
- white glue (optional)

Set 1 pie pan right-side up on table. Turn second pie pan upside down and place on top of first pan. Staple rims of both pie pans together.

Decorate saucer like a space ship. Color windows and door with felt pen or glue felt cut-outs in place. Soar saucer by holding rims with fingers. A flip of the wrist sends the saucer soaring into space. (See figure 1-1a.)

figure 1-1a   *Soaring Saucer viewed by Krinkled Kritter (See page 22.)*

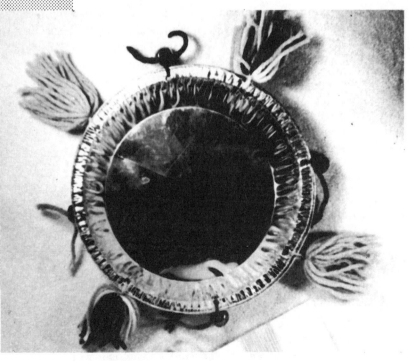

figure 1-1b   *Tambourine*

teaching tips

Children can toss saucers inside or outside. Have a contest! See who can soar their saucer the farthest distance or come closest to a predetermined spot.

Transform saucer into a musical instrument by dropping a few small pebbles, uncooked rice or dried beans in bottom pan before joining rims. Then, with paper punch, make 8 evenly spaced holes around rim of joined pans. Tie bells and yarn fringe in holes. (See figure 1-1b.) Tambourine can also be painted with tempera. Add a few drops of liquid dishwashing detergent or vinegar to paint so that it will adhere to the aluminum.

evaluation

Agreement of parts of the design with each other; and skill in use of color as complete work is painted.

[*Note: where pupil evaluation is required, you may apply the suggestions in the evaluation sections that accompany each craft activity.*]

Winter Wonderland

—just a spoonful of moth flakes makes this toy enchanting!

materials

- 1 baby food jar with lid (washed, dried and label removed)
- water
- white glue
- 5-minute epoxy glue
- scissors
- miniature figurine
- black felt-tipped pen (kind that writes on anything)
- moth flakes (found in most variety stores)
- popsicle stick
- measuring spoon
- plastic coffee can lid
- felt scraps
- scraps of lace or decorative trim

Remove lid from jar. Place lid upside down on felt scrap, and trace it. Cut out felt circle.

Test figurine to make sure it fits inside baby food jar. Use popsicle stick to mix small amount of 5-minute epoxy glue in coffee can lid. Follow glue directions. Spread glue over bottom of figurine. Set figurine inside jar lid; center figurine and press down firmly. Let glue dry. (If you do not use 5-minute epoxy glue, allow glue to dry 24 hours before proceeding.)

Drop 1 heaping teaspoon of moth flakes into baby food jar. Fill jar with water to almost overflowing. Mix another small batch of epoxy glue and spread around inside edge of jar lid. Push figurine into water filled jar and screw lid on tightly. If water overflows, wipe away any moth flakes between lid and jar edge for a water-proof seal. Let glue dry.

Use white glue to attach felt circle to outside of jar lid. Turn jar upside down. Glue lace or decorative trim around neck of jar; trim should be wide enough to cover sides of jar lid. Allow glue to dry. Now, shake jar gently and watch it snow up a storm! (See figure 1-2.)

figure 1-2   *Winter Wonderland sits atop Marble Paperweight (left) and Flowery Fantasy (right).*

teaching tips

The only problem with this craft is the glue just doesn't seem to dry fast enough for excited children.

Transforming this Winter Wonderland into perennial spring is easy. Crinkle a small amount of plastic wrap between your hands and stuff it into a baby food jar. Push a small cluster of artificial flowers (upside down) into jar and fill with water to brim.

Tint the water with a few drops of food coloring. Smear 5-minute epoxy glue around inside edge of jar lid and screw lid on tightly. Let glue dry. Decorate lid with lace or color lid with black felt-tipped pen. Turn jar upside down for a perfect paperweight!

This handy idea also makes a dandy Father's Day' gift. Fill clean jar with marbles. Glue on lid and decorate with braid or rick-rack.

evaluation

Pupil workmanship; decoration; lack of air space inside jar; neatness; and originality.

Snow Pictures in July

—creamy, synthetic snow makes oodles of fun!

materials

- 1 can nonmentholated shaving cream
- wax paper
- bowl of water
- food coloring (all colors)
- old newspaper

Cover play surface with newspaper. Place sheets of wax paper over newspaper. Ooze mountains of shaving cream onto wax paper. Let the kids dive in with hands and fingers to create snowy scenes.

Brighten up the fun by dropping a few drops of food coloring into shaving cream. As "snow" begins to dry, rejuvenate with a few drops of water. (See figure 1-3.)

teaching tips

Shaving cream used like finger paint is a fascinating, inexpensive media. Some supervision is required for this craft since shaving cream should not be put in the students' eyes or mouths. Mentholated shaving cream is not recommended since it may burn if accidentally put in the eyes.

Children can create in small groups or individually; and clean-up is no

figure 1-3   *Snow Pictures in July!*

problem since students simply roll up the cream-covered paper and throw it in the trash. And, when they wash their hands, they will give the sink a good scrubbing!

evaluation

Creativity of designs; originality; imagination; and use of color.

Super Summer Scoopers

—unbreakable toys for classroom or playground fun!

materials

- 2 ½-gallon plastic jugs with lids
- smooth-edged knife (or sharp scissors)
- black crayon
- ruler
- felt-tipped pens (kinds that write on anything)
- paper towels
- liquid detergent

Rinse out jug with warm soapy water. Remove label; wash and dry jug. If the label glue refuses to budge, scrape it off gently with a knife or pot scrubber.

Place the jug in your lap—handle to the back—front facing you, with top toward your knees. Use ruler to measure about 5″ up from the bottom of the jug. (Most jugs already have a pressed line around this area.) Place ruler at top of 5″ line. Draw a 4″ line across front of jug. This is the basic scoop shape.

At each end of the 4″ line, draw a 5″ line down each side of the jug, curving top corners. Slightly curve lines at base of jug. Continue crayon line all the way around the top edge of the bottom of the jug. (Bottom will be cut away entirely.) Carefully cut along crayon line. Throw away jug scraps. Trim uneven lines with scissors.

Decorate scooper with felt-tipped pens. Using the handle as a nose, draw big eyes on scooper or adorn with pictures of flowers, birds or sea shells.

Play ball inside with super scoopers. Stand 2 students face to face, a few feet apart from each other. They can toss and catch a small rubber ball or fluffy nylon net scrubber inside (directions for Nylon Net Scrubber on page 159); or students can play with a tennis ball outside. (See figure 1-4.)

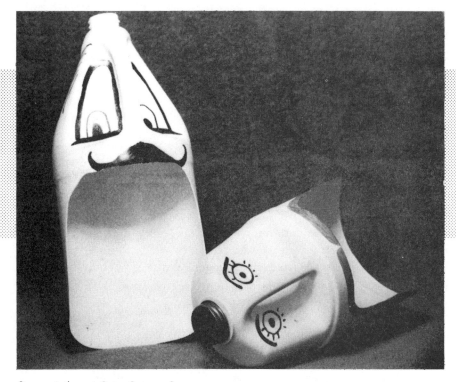

figure 1-4   *Super Summer Scoopers*

teaching tips

Scoopers should be pre-cut for students in kindergarten through fourth grade. Older students can cut their own scoopers with supervision. Since fifth- and sixth-graders have larger hands, let them make scoopers out of gallon jugs. (Opening will be approximately 7″ long by 6″ wide.)

Super scoopers also make excellent sand box diggers for young students.

evaluation

Kindergarten through fourth grade—quality of decoration art.

Fifth and sixth grades—basic scoop shape; cutting ability; and quality of decoration.

Differences in pupil motor skills and coordination during play.

Krinkled Kritters

—sparkling kritters from crushed aluminum foil!

materials

- aluminum foil
- felt scraps
- paper punch
- pipe cleaners
- white glue
- scraps of construction paper (optional)
- tempera paint (optional)
- paint brush (optional)
- liquid detergent (optional)

Tear a sheet of aluminum foil off roll. Crush foil with hands. Shape into an animal form. Glue felt (or paper) eyes, ears, nose, etc. on kritter.

Use pipe cleaners to make legs, antennae and tail. Cover body with paper punch felt spots and other shapes. (See figure 1-5a.)

teaching tips

Attach a string to spider kritter and dangle from ceiling, or make a bird by gluing on feathers or black bats with construction paper wings. Stick broom straw whiskers into kitty cat and perch it on a rock. (See figure 1-5b.)

figure 1-5a   *Krinkled Kritters*

figure 1-5b   *Krinkled Kritter Kat*

evaluation

Originality; imagination; facial features; shapes; perspective; and overall craft.

Cagey Classroom Zoo

—a visit to the zoo is as close as a shoe box!

materials

- 1 empty shoe box (without lid)
- large 2-eye button
- paste (or white glue)
- crayons (or tempera paint or felt-tipped pens)
- scissors
- string (or yarn)
- ruler
- poster board (or heavy paper)
- old magazines (or coloring books or greeting cards)
- cellophane tape
- compass point

Draw a zoo animal on heavy paper or cut out an animal picture from a magazine, coloring book or greeting card. Glue thin pictures to heavy paper or poster board backing. (Animal should be 2″ shorter than the inside height of the shoe box.) Tape a piece of string, 2″ longer than the shoe box height, to the back of the animal cut-out. Set animal inside.

Turn the shoe box up on one long side. (The bottom of the box becomes the back of the zoo cage.) Draw and color background inside shoe box. Picture should resemble the animal's natural habitat.

Next, punch a hole through the middle of the top of the box. Set the animal cut-out inside the box and thread loose end of string up through hole. Tie button to string to prevent it from slipping back into cage. Button allows students to maneuver their puppet-like, caged animal.

Cut 10 or 12 strips of string (or yarn) for bars of cage. The string should be long enough to tape across the front top and bottom of box. Use ruler to space strings evenly across the top front of box. Tape strings in place. Pull strings down across front of box, one at a time, and tape to the underside of box. Decorate outside of box if desired. (See figure 1-6.)

figure 1-6   *Cagey Classroom Zoo*

teaching tips

Make a complete zoo. Each student can choose one animal so the finished zoo will have a nice variety. Line up animal cages or place them in a semicircle for classroom exhibition.

Students can research their animals and share their knowledge with classmates during "Show and Tell." To store, stack cages on top of one another.

evaluation

Realism of animal and habitat; creativity; imagination; neatness; spacing of cage bars; and background design and coloring.

Rainy Day Ring Toss

—indoor horsehoe-like game tosses rainy day blues away!

materials

- 1 tall, round cardboard canister (kind potato chips come in)
- sand (or small pebbles)
- self-adhesive backed paper (or construction paper)

- white glue (optional)
- scissors
- ruler
- dark crayon
- 1 gallon plastic jug (with label removed)
- felt-tipped marking pens (kinds that write on anything)

Remove plastic lid from canister. Decorate outside by covering with self-adhesive backed paper or glue on construction paper. Fill decorated canister with sand (or pebbles). Snap on lid.

Make 3 1"-wide rings from gallon plastic jug. Decorate rings with felt-tipped pens. To play, place canister in center of room. Toss rings at canister much like throwing horseshoes. Students can play for fun or points. (See figure 1-7.)

figure 1-7   *Rainy Day Ring Ross*

teaching tips

Pre-cut rings for young students.
Hook rings together with a pipe cleaner for storage.

evaluation

Decoration of canister; cutting of rings; and overall decoration.

Play Peanut Pachyderm

—little elephant provides a trunk full of fun!

materials

- poster board
- felt-tipped pens (or crayons)
- scissors
- 11″ piece of string
- compass point (or bent paper clip)
- paper nut cup (found in variety or stationery stores)
- tracing paper
- pencil

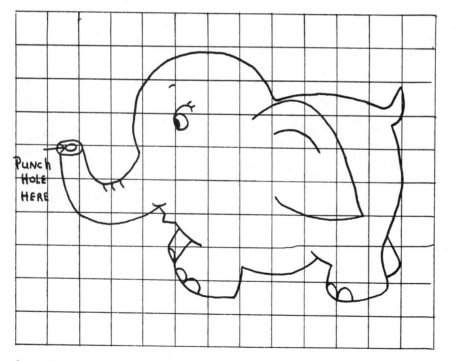

PUNCH
HOLE
HERE

figure 1-8a   *Pattern for Play Peanut Pachyderm*

First, enlarge elephant pattern (figure 1-8a) according to general instructions for enlarging patterns in the following section.

This pattern and others in this book are drawn to scale and may be constructed in actual size by redrawing outlines on paper ruled with ½" squares. Paper that is already squared may be purchased at an office supply or stationery store, or you can draw your own. Draw lines ½" apart on plain paper; then, carefully copy lines of pattern in each corresponding square. To avoid confusion, try numbering each square both vertically and horizontally from left to right, matching squares by counting so many numbers across and down—rather like a crossword puzzle. Students can trace your enlarged pattern or you can have extra copies run off on an office copying machine.

Trace elephant pattern on poster board and cut out; color body and facial features. Use compass point to make a small hole in the tip of the elephant's trunk. Slip string through hole, and tie in a knot. Punch another hole in nut cup side near the top. Push other end of string through cup and tie.

Now hold elephant in one hand and, using wrist action, flip up nut cup and catch it with the elephant's trunk. (See figure 1-8b.)

figure 1-8b   *Play Peanut Pachyderm*

teaching tips

Prepare elephant pattern in advance for young students, and they may also need help tying their knots.

Older students can dream up other animals, such as a ring-tailed monkey or a big-horned rhinoceros.

evaluation

Cutting; coloring; neatness; and differences in pupil motor skills and coordination during play.

chapter two —

Paper Potpourri

Nothing will ever replace paper as a classroom favorite. Children love to draw, color, cut, feel and shape paper. And, you will appreciate the convenience of these crafts since paper supplies are always close at hand.

Educational values in this chapter include perspective, color coordination, cutting, manual dexterity, imagination, design and shapes.

Valentine Cut-Up

—puzzling valentine, fun to make or receive!

materials

- poster board
- felt-tipped pens (or crayons)
- scissors
- construction paper
- rubber cement (or paste)
- pencil
- tall, round cardboard canister (kind potato chips come in)
- old magazines and greeting cards (optional)

Quarter poster board. (1 board will make 4 puzzles.) Draw a Valentine picture and message on poster board, and color. Young students can glue cut out magazine pictures or pieces of greeting cards in place.

Turn poster board over. Draw a puzzle design on the back, and cut out puzzle pieces. Each piece should be small enough to fit inside cardboard canister.

When puzzle is complete, decorate canister with construction paper; cover canister completely. Glue hearts and cupids, cut from construction paper or old greeting cards, on covered canister; and decorate lid.

Drop puzzle pieces into canister, and snap on lid. Give scrambled-up message to a favorite Valentine and let him or her put the pieces together. (See figure 2-1.)

figure 2-1   *Valentine Cut-Up*

teaching tips

Do not cut sample puzzle into pieces until students can study puzzle piece shapes.

Let young students make small puzzles since their hands tire easily from cutting.

Cut-ups make delightful holiday gifts. Just change the puzzle picture to suit the occasion.

evaluation

Artwork; puzzle design; cutting; canister decoration; originality; imagination; and neatness.

Punchy Pictures

—big and little pictures from dots!

materials

- paper punch
- heavy construction paper (or poster board or old greeting cards)
- white glue (or rubber cement)
- fine-pointed, felt-tipped pens
- toothpick
- pencil
- black yarn (optional)
- plain white paper
- butter tubs (with lids)

Punch out dots from construction paper, poster board or greeting cards. Punch 1 color of dots at a time over butter or margarine tub (with lid removed). During gluing, sprinkle dots from tub onto lid for easy access. Snap on lid for storage. Glue colored dots on construction paper to create pictures and cards like a Halloween jack-o-lantern. (See figure 2-2a.)

figure 2-2a   *Punchy Pictures*

Create dot mosaics and abstract art by outlining design with black yarn glued in place. When yarn is dry, glue dots inside lines 1 at a time.

Make fancy stationery and recipe cards by decorating plain paper and index cards with miniature punchy pictures—1 red dot makes a red apple; 1 brown dot becomes a baby owl; 3 dots make swimming fishes; black dots become musical

figure 2-2b   *Punchy Picture stationery, note pads and recipe*
cards

notes; 4 dots stacked on top of each other make a totem pole; 1 green dot becomes a turtle; and 4 dots join to form a spotted caterpillar. (See figure 2-2b.)

To make stationery pretty, lightly sketch miniature design on paper. Color background with fine-pointed, felt-tipped pens. Then, glue dots in place and add final touches.

teaching tips

When gluing large pictures, smear glue on a small area of the picture. Press dots in glue 1 at a time. (A toothpick will help dot stick to glue instead of your finger.)

Utilize coloring books for basic picture and mosaic designs.

Colorful little dots also can be glued to hard boiled eggs at Easter time. Dots on blown-out eggs can be varnished and will last indefinitely.

evaluation

Use of color; originality of design, neatness; artwork; and overall project.

Storybook Masks

—paper personalities add to storytelling and classroom plays.

materials

- poster board (or heavy cardboard)
- construction paper
- thin elastic or rubber band (optional)
- stapler (optional)
- crayons (or felt-tipped pens)
- rubber cement (or paste)
- scissors
- pencil

Sketch animal or character head on poster board. (Color of poster board should be the same as the animal's basic body color—brown wolf, yellow chick, green alligator, etc.)

Cut out head. Draw and cut out construction paper eyes, mouth, etc., and glue features on animal head. If cardboard is used, cover it with construction paper or paint with tempera before gluing on facial features. Hold mask in front of face when acting out story. (See figure 2-3.)

figure 2-3   *Storybook Masks*

teaching tips

Students can tape a stick near the bottom on the back of the mask for easy holding, or they can punch a hole in each side and insert thin elastic (or a broken rubber band) and staple to hold mask in place.

Eye slots are not required for hold-up masks, but they are necessary for those held in place with elastic.

Make small masks and tape to unsharpened pencils for miniature storybook puppets.

evaluation

Mask shape; design; facial features; proportion; and originality.

Spring Floral Plaques

—tiny treasures to set in an easel or string on a wall.

materials

- any color poster board
- florist clay (or strong tape)
- pencil
- white glue
- 1 plastic egg carton
- artificial or dried flowers and ferns
- pull ring (with tab removed) from juice or soda can
- ribbon (optional)
- a 3", 4-pronged curtain pleater hook (optional)

Make basic plaque pattern from scrap poster board. (See figure 2-4a.) To enlarge pattern, see page 28. Place pattern shape on poster board, outline and cut out. Remove lid from egg carton, and cut out 1 egg cup section. Cut section in half to create flower vase.

Pinch off a ball of florist clay (about the size of your thumb), and press clay on plaque about 1" up from the bottom. Make sure clay is centered. Press artificial or dried flowers into clay, 1 at a time.

When flowers are in place, pinch off another piece of clay (about the size of your baby finger), and press this clay on top of the flower stems. (If you don't have clay, hold flowers in one hand and wrap tape around the stems; then tape flowers to plaque.)

Run a bead of glue around the cut edges of the egg section vase. Place the vase on top of the flower stems. (Vase will hide stems.) Stand floral plaque up on an easel or attach a pretty ribbon and hang it on the wall.

To make Easy Easel, hold 3", 4-pronged curtain hook in your hand, and turn

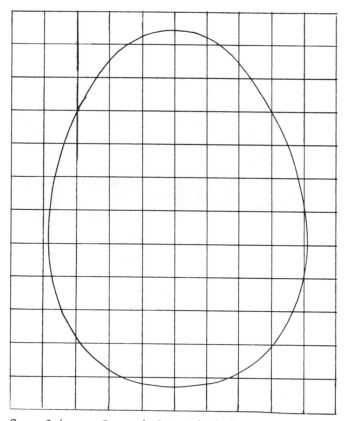

figure 2-4a   *Pattern for Spring Floral Plaque*

it upside down. (Hanging hook will be turned up.) Pull the 2 inside prongs toward you and the 2 outside prongs away from you. It's that easy! Test the easel by setting it on a table to make sure it is level. Then set floral plaque on curved hanging hook. Shove hook through the bottom of the vase to secure.

To make Ribbon Hang-Up, cut a piece of grosgrain (or velvet) ribbon 8" long. Slip ribbon through a soda can pull ring (with tab removed). Fold ribbon in half and tape (or staple) ribbon ends to back of plaque. Make sure flowers hide the staple.

Hang 2 or 3 plaques on 1 long streamer of ribbon. Tape ribbon streamers on the lower bottom of plaque if desired. (See figure 2-4b.)

teaching tips

Plaques can be made in various shapes and sizes. Circles, squares, rectangles and even coffee can lids work nicely. Students can initial their artwork upon completion for a more professional look.

Floral designs can be brightened up with glitter, tiny bumblebees or butter-

figure 2-4b   *Spring Floral Plaques—Easy Easel and Ribbon Hang-Up*

flies. Sea shells can also be glued to basic plaque for an underwater scene. Glue a small strip of nylon net over completed picture for added effect.

evaluation

Plaque shape in relation to floral arrangement; use of color; balance; design; and originality.

Rainy Day Zots

—black spots make you name it zots!

materials

- heavy white paper (Typing paper works nicely.)
- indelible black ink

- black construction paper (optional)
- paper plate (optional)
- felt-tipped marking pens or crayons (optional)
- glue (optional)
- scissors (optional)
- old newspaper
- apron (or old shirt)

Cover work area with newspaper, and don apron. Lay 1 piece of white paper on top of newspaper, fold paper in half, and then re-open.

Use ink bottle dropper to drop ink on ½ of paper. Quickly fold paper in half (along fold line) and press with palm of hand. Open paper. If zot design is not to your liking, add a few more drops of ink and repeat the process.

Glue 2″ strips of black construction paper around edges of zot picture for a border, or cut out design and glue it inside a paper plate. Decorate outside edges with felt-tipped pens or crayons.

Glue trimmed zot designs to stationery box top or around a tin can to dress them up, or create zot animals and add movable eyes or construction paper facial features. (See figure 2-5.)

figure 2-5   *Rainy Day Zots*

teaching tips

Indelible ink is waterproof, so care should be taken to protect clothes, carpeting and table tops.

Use different colors of ink to make zany zot wrapping paper from white freezer paper, or glue cut-outs on newsprint to create a wall mural.

Young students can soak a sheet of paper in a pan of water. Place paper on old newspaper and quickly drop water colors (or tempera paint or food coloring) onto paper. Reaction will cause paint and water to create rainbow zots. Let paper dry before displaying.

evaluation

Neatness; design; imagination; and decorative use of completed craft.

Tammy Turtle

—upside-down paper plate makes a whimsical creature!

materials

- paper plate
- crayons
- construction paper
- string (optional)
- pencil
- tracing paper
- scissors
- white glue (or stapler)
- thin cardboard (The side of a detergent box works nicely.)

Make pattern pieces from thin cardboard. (See figure 2-6a.) Refer to page 28 to enlarge pattern. Trace pattern pieces on construction paper, and cut out. Set plate right side up and glue (or staple) turtle parts in place—upside down.

Turn plate over and draw turtle shell design on paper plate bottom. Color shell; then draw facial features on turtle head. (See figure 2-6b.)

teaching tips

Take Tammy for a stroll by punching a hole through the shell near the head and inserting a pull string.

Older students will prefer to make a Tammy bank from a colorful plastic margarine tub. Cut pattern pieces from heavy poster board. (See figure 2-6c.) Use pattern-enlarging techniques on page 28. Draw a mouth and glue a wiggly eye (or button) on each side of the head; then turn the margarine tub upside down and rest it on the lid.

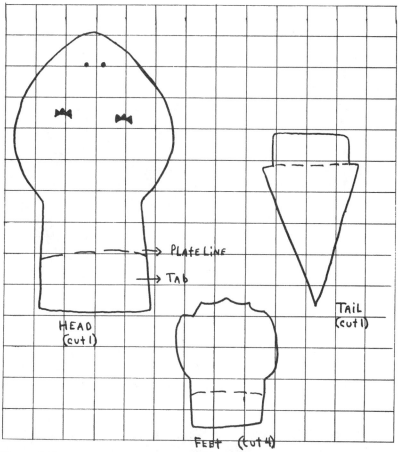

PLATE LINE

TAB

HEAD (cut 1)

TAIL (cut 1)

FEET (cut 4)

figure 2-6a   *Pattern pieces for Tammy Turtle*

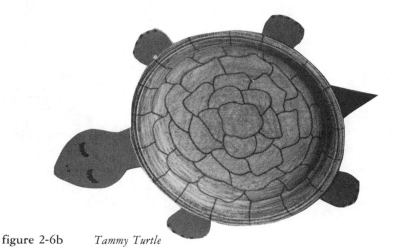

figure 2-6b   *Tammy Turtle*

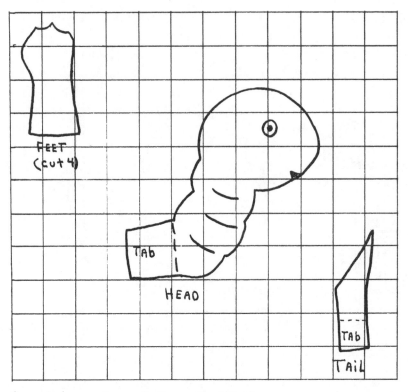

FEET
(cut 4)

TAB

HEAD

TAB

TAIL

figure 2-6c   *Pattern for Tammy Turtle Bank*

figure 2-6d   *Tammy Turtle Bank*

Use a safety razor blade (or knife) to cut a coin slot in the center bottom of tub. Next, make a single slit in the tub where the head will go. Turn the tub a half circle and make a small slit for the tail.

Turn the tub right side up. Glue or tape turtle feet on lid—upside down. Turn the tub to upright position and insert head and tail in slots. Leave Tammy plain or dress with scraps of lace, rick-rack, fringe balls or felt flowers. (See figure 2-6d.)

Close supervision is necessary when cutting, or you might prefer to cut all tub slots in advance.

evaluation

Both crafts for design; neatness; facial features; and originality.

Ecology Week Wastepaper Basket

—decorative, handy trash basket from paper scraps!

materials

- colorful magazine pictures (minus printed words)
- ½" wooden dowel stick
- white glue
- clear varnish
- paint brush
- enamel spray paint (any color)
- scissors
- white plastic clothesline
- rubber bands
- round, 5-gallon ice cream carton
- old newspaper

Cover work area with newspaper. Set ice cream carton on newspaper and spray inside of carton with enamel paint. (Paint only in a well-ventilated area.) Set painted carton aside to dry.

Cut white border off colorful magazine pictures unless you want a striped basket. Lay colored side of picture face down on a flat surface. Place dowel stick (or large knitting needle) on 1 corner, and roll picture around dowel stick. Dot end corner of paper with glue. Then remove dowel stick. Continue rolling until you have approximately 100 rolled pictures.

When glue on rolls is dry, measure 1 roll the length of container. Be sure bottom of roll is below carton's metal rim.

Cut all rolls the proper length. Spread a small amount of glue on 1 section of container at a time, and lay rolled pictures in glue. (It's easier to lay carton on its side for gluing process.) Continue gluing rolls in place until entire carton is covered. Keep rolls straight. When carton is covered, secure rolls with rubber bands until glue dries.

Varnish outside of basket, and let dry. Now, cut white clothesline into 3″ strips. Insert 1 strip into the first and fourth hole of magazine rolls; begin anywhere at top of container. Place a second strip in second hole, and skip 2 holes and insert other end of strip. Continue until top of basket is laced with clothesline strips.

Insert strips in the same manner around bottom of basket.

teaching tips

A classroom demonstration will help students catch on to this activity. All students will be able to roll their pictures, but young students will need help cutting and inserting clothesline strips.

Personalize baskets for Mom or Dad by gluing paper or felt monograms on the front.

Students can also make matching items. Use a 2-lb. coffee can for a letter

figure 2-7   *Ecology Week Wastepaper Basket, Letter holder and Pencil holder*

holder and approximately 50 magazine pictures, and make a pencil holder from a frozen juice can and 25 pictures. You may or may not choose to paint the inside of the containers. (See figure 2-7.)

evaluation

Neatness; color coordination; uniformity of rolled pictures; gluing; placement of clothesline; and overall, completed craft.

chapter three —

Mother Hubbard's Cupboard

Unlike the legendary title character, the average kitchen cupboard is stuffed with a bounty of craft supplies.

This chapter is a lesson in ingenuity and economics, teaching students to turn ordinary materials into extraordinary crafts. Encourage students to bring supplies from home and share them.

Educational values in this chapter include design, color coordination, perspective, proportion, physical and manual dexterity, shapes and spatial relations.

Crunchy Mosaics

—realistic, 3-dimensional pictures from breakfast cereal!

materials

- construction paper
- lightweight cardboard (optional)
- white glue
- black yarn (optional)
- felt-tipped marking pens (or crayons)
- scissors
- assortment of breakfast cereal
- wiggly eyes (optional)
- buttons (optional)
- coloring books (or used greeting cards)
- tracing paper (optional)

- plastic margarine tubs (to contain cereal)
- pencil
- cotton swab
- old newspapers

Select a picture of an animal from a coloring book or greeting card. Cover work area with newspaper. Draw or trace a picture on a sheet of construction paper, and outline picture with felt-tipped pen, dark crayon or glue black yarn in place. Let glued yarn dry before proceeding.

Squeeze glue on a small section of the picture at a time, and spread it inside lines with a cotton swab. Sprinkle or place cereal in glue. Continue working until entire picture is covered. Let glue dry.

Turn picture upside down and shake gently to remove excess cereal. Then touch up bald spots. Glue wiggly or button eyes in place, and complete picture by drawing and coloring background scene. (See figure 3-1a.)

figure 3-1a   *Crunchy Mosaics—elephant is outlined in black yarn before cereal is glued in place.*

teaching tips

Select cereal that will enhance students' pictures. For white lambs and rabbits, substitute unbuttered and unsalted popcorn for cereal.

Pictures outlined with yarn will be easier projects for students in kindergarten through second grade. The outline takes more time, but it will be easier for them to apply the cereal within the lines.

To make a stand-up picture, draw an animal and outline with pen or crayon. Cut out the animal leaving about a 2"-thick border along the bottom. Cover animal with cereal and color background.

Make a ½" slit in the center bottom of the cut-out. Cut a strip of cardboard about 2½" × 1", and cut a ½" slit in the center of this strip. Insert the small strip slit into the slit of animal cut-out. Adjust until animal stands up. (See figure 3-1b.) Stand-up animals should be made on poster board or sturdy cardboard for best results.

figure 3-1b   *Crunchy Mosaic Stand-Up—note small white strip of cardboard in foreground inserted in slot in center of animal picture to permit monkey to stand up.*

evaluation

Selection of picture and appropriateness of cereal; background art and coloring; gluing; closeness of cereal; originality; neatness; and overall, completed craft.

April Marsh Rabbits

—puffy white bunnies good enough to eat!

materials

- 3 large marshmallows
- 5 toothpicks (wooden)
- scissors
- cellophane tape
- pink construction paper
- small chocolate candy bar
- electric hot plate (or make your own—directions on page 67)
- small tin can (A tuna fish can works nicely.)
- wax paper

Cover work area with wax paper. Wash and dry tuna fish can, and remove label. Break up chocolate candy and drop in can.

Stick 1 toothpick in 1 marshmallow. Slide second marshmallow on toothpick to form basic rabbit shape. Cut 2 rabbit ears from construction paper. Break 1 toothpick in half, and tape 1 ear to each toothpick half. Stick ears in top marshmallow.

Cut remaining marshmallow in quarters. Use a piece of toothpick to stick on 1 quarter and push tail in place. Melt chocolate over low heat. Use a toothpick to paint facial features on rabbit.

figure 3-2   *April Marsh Rabbits*

Fill miniature Easter baskets with April Marsh Rabbits, sit tasty treat atop a cookie, or make a batch of bunnies to decorate a classroom cake. (See figure 3-2.)

teaching tips

Care should be taken to remove all toothpicks before students eat their rabbits.

Create baby marsh rabbits from miniature marshmallows.

evaluation

Size and proportion of rabbit ears; facial features; and originality.

Crazy Crackles

—delicate mosaic designs from dried egg shells!

materials

- empty egg shells
- bleach (optional)
- glass jar (optional)
- wax paper
- black enamel spray paint
- white glue (Be sure it dries clear.)
- old newspapers
- toothpick (or pick-up stick)
- heavy paper plate (optional)
- assorted colors of acrylic paint (optional)
- black tempera paint (optional)
- ½" paint brush
- cotton swab
- paper towels
- any size sturdy container (like a small candy can, cookie tin, cigar box, wood or metal recipe box, old vase or serving tray)
- plastic margarine tub

Rinse egg shells well, and dry with paper towels. (Pack discolored or dirty egg shells in a glass jar. Cover with bleach and let soak overnight. Rinse bleached shells well, and spread on paper towels to dry.) Cover work area with newspaper. In a well-ventilated area, spray container with black enamel paint; let dry.

Cover table or flat surface with wax paper, and spread out dry egg shells. Set container on table. Break shells into pieces about the size of your thumb. Squeeze glue on 1 section of the container at a time. Spread glue with fingers or use a cotton swab.

One at a time, place pieces of egg shell (concave side down) in glue. With toothpick, press down on shell until it cracks into smaller pieces. (See figure 3-3a.) (You can also use a pick-up stick, blunt-ended needle or tear a piece of wax paper off and put it on top of the shell and crack with fingers.)

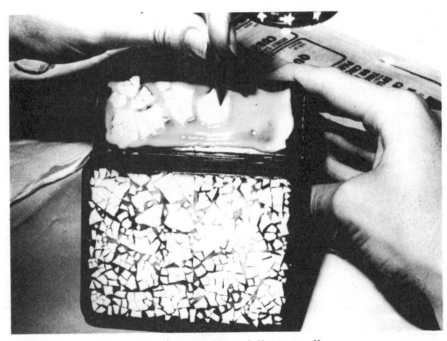

figure 3-3a   *Crazy Crackles—crackling shell into small pieces with a toothpick*

Continue process of gluing shells on container and cracking until outside is completely covered. Fill in any open areas with small shell chips—a toothpick will help here. Let glue dry. Now, squeeze a small amount of glue into the margarine tub, add a few drops of water and mix. Paint mixture over glued shells. Let dry. Apply a second coat for good coverage.

Students can glue a felt or fabric lining inside container. Crackled box can hold jewelry, coins or be set on a coffee table for display. (See figure 3-3b.)

figure 3-3b   *Small candy can becomes a decorative box.*

teaching tips

The amount of shells required depends upon the size of the container to be covered.

Glue shells close together, but not overlapping. Shells should be glued concave side down for easier cracking; however, students can glue shells curved side up for a different effect.

Students in the fourth through sixth grades will enjoy the challenge and end result of this activity. Kindergarten through third-graders might find the shell application tedious, but they can make their own crazy crackles by applying shells (any which way) to a painted paper plate.

Smear glue on inside bottom of plate and press in shells. Cover entire bottom, and let glue dry. Paint shells with acrylic to produce unusual or colorful designs. (See figure 3-3c.)

Grind dried egg shells into mosaic gravel by placing shells between 2 layers of wax paper and crush with a rolling pin. Fill 4 or 5 baby food jars with crushed shells. Squirt a few drops of food coloring into jar; screw on lid, and shake well. Spread colored shell gravel on waxed paper to dry.

Students can make mosaic pictures, such as those outlined on page 48, by substituting gravel for cereal. Paint finished gravel picture with a mixture of glue and water to preserve and brighten colors.

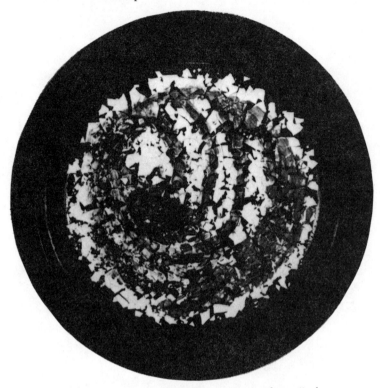

figure 3-3c   *Cracy Crackles hatch into a "far out" abstract
picture when glued on a paper plate.*

evaluation

Crackled container—uniformity of egg shell pieces; application of shells; painting; neatness; originality; and aesthetic appeal of completed craft.

Paper plate—basic paint coverage; application of shells; neatness; painted artwork; and completed craft.

Quality of crushed shell mosaics (according to guidelines on page 52).

Holiday-Roni Tree

—tall, golden table decoration or mantel ornament!

materials

- old newspapers
- white glue
- tall, stemmed glass (like a wine goblet)
- assortment of macaroni in various shapes and sizes

- gold spray paint
- plastic coffee can lid
- scissors
- paper or cloth tape

Spread 3 sheets of double-paged newspaper on the floor (or large table). Make a cone shape. (See figure 3-4a.) Roll corner A toward corner B; when half the cone is shaped, roll toward corner C. Stick a piece of tape at the top of the shaped cone. Cut off excess paper at bottom of cone.

Sit the large, open end of the cone over the glass or tall vase or bottle with pedestal base. (See figure 3-4b.) Fit the glass snugly inside the cone with only the stem and base showing.

Adjust the cone until it fits the glass. Put your hand inside the cone and twist to make it larger or smaller. Keep testing until the glass fits snugly inside. Tape the outside edges of the newspaper cone. Tape inside edges of the cone so it will not unwind.

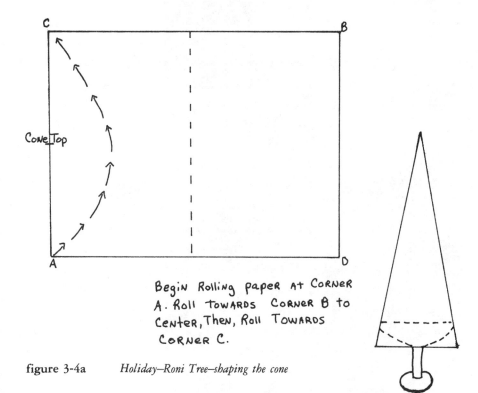

Begin Rolling paper At Corner A. Roll towards Corner B to Center, Then, Roll Towards Corner C.

figure 3-4a   *Holiday–Roni Tree–shaping the cone*

figure 3-4b   *Fitting cone to glass*

Adjust Cone until it Fits Snugly inside glass.

A nice-sized cone is 14″ to 16″ tall. Make smaller cones by trimming more newspaper off bottom before fitting cone to glass. You will also need to adjust the size of the glass in proportion to size of the cone.

Sit glass in a safe place. Cover work area with newspaper. Squeeze glue into coffee can lid, and pour an assortment of macaroni out on table. With fingers, spread a generous amount of glue on 1 section of cone at a time. Start at the bottom and work upward.

Stick macaroni into glue 1 at a time. Alternate macaroni shapes and sizes for best results. Cover as much of the cone as possible for a pretty tree. (See figure 3-4c.) Continue gluing on macaroni until entire tree is covered. Put fancy bow-shaped macaroni on top of the complete tree and you can glue a border of bows around the bottom.

figure 3-4c   *Gluing macaroni on newspaper cone*

Place tree on glass and let dry overnight. In a well-ventilated area, spray tree, glass base and stem with gold paint or any color you like. Let dry. (See figure 3-4d.)

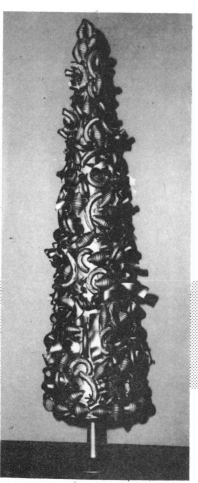

figure 3-4d   *Holiday–Roni Tree*

teaching tips

Students can work on their trees a little each day. Slip tree on glass when not working and set in a safe place.

The newspaper cone keeps the cost of this craft nominal. Foam cones can be used, but they must be sprayed with a special paint to keep them from dissolving.

Kindergarten through third-graders can make ice cream cone trees or glue macaroni to a cigar box top or plastic margarine tub lid for tricky trinket boxes. Or, glue macaroni to a cardboard picture frame or to a paper towel tube roll candle.

Ask students to bring a glass and macaroni shapes from home the day before you begin.

evaluation

Shape and size of newspaper cone; placement of macaroni; coverage; use of macaroni to produce designs; originality; and spray painting.

Strung-Out Spuds

—diced-up potatoes, dried and strung, make unique jewelry for everyone!

materials

- a large, firm potato
- potato peeler
- cutting board
- knife
- tapestry needle
- thick cotton string (The kind used to fly kites works nicely.)
- old beans (or buttons)
- thin elastic cord (optional)
- acrylic paint (optional)
- paint brush (optional)
- fine fishing line (or super strength polyester thread)
- jewelry jump ring (optional)
- needle nose pliers (optional)
- narrow leather cord (or rug yarn—optional)
- old newspapers
- paper towels
- large-eyed needle

Cover work area with newspaper. Peel skin from potato, and dice potato into small cubes (approximately ½" square). Thread tapestry needle with thick string. Tie a knot in 1 end of string, and thread potato squares on string. Push needle through the center of each potato. Continue until all potato squares are strung.

Hang strung-out spuds in a well-ventilated (preferably warm) area to dry. Depending upon the weather, it will take approximately 10 days for potato squares to dry. (They will shrink, get very hard and turn dark gray or black when dry.)

Pull dry potatoes from string. Thread a large-eyed needle with a long, double strand of heavy duty thread (or fishing line). Knot ends of thread.

String potato squares on thread, adding beads (or buttons) for color and decoration. Make sure thread is long enough to slip over your head so you won't need a necklace clasp. (See figure 3-5a.)

figure 3-5a   *Strung-Out Spuds make a perfectly original necklace.*

figure 3-5b   *Strung-Out Spud Medallion—freshly cut potato cubes to right of medallion dry to produce materials for this unusual craft.*

Girls, and especially boys, will enjoy making strung out medallions. String beads and spuds on 9″ of double thread; leave 1″ for tying off ends. Use needle nose pliers to slip a jump ring around the thread and attach to a leather cord. Tie cord ends to complete slip-over-the-head medallion. (See figure 3-5b.)

teaching tips

No one will believe these hard, stone-like jewels are dried potatoes!

Dried spuds can be painted with acrylic before or after stringing.

Students can make their own beads to decorate their necklace. (See fruit dough recipe on page 185.) Mix dough and pinch off a piece about the size of your thumb, and roll dough into ball. Make a hole in center with toothpick (or tapestry needle). Let dough dry. Paint dried beads with acrylic (or fingernail polish) and let dry before stringing. For shiny beads, coat with varnish or clear fingernail polish.

evaluation

Cutting of potato squares; assembly and arrangement of necklace; originality; use of color; design; and aesthetic appeal of completed jewelry.

Tin Can Personalities

—imagination and paint transform old cans into decorative personalities!

materials

- empty aluminum soft drink cans
- black enamel spray paint
- small paint brushes
- 1 bottle white paint (enamel, acrylic or tempera)
- 1 bottle black enamel paint (kind used to paint model cars and airplanes)
- 4″ × 4″ tile squares (or wooden blocks)
- varnish (optional)
- ½″ paint brush (optional)
- pipe cleaners
- ball point pen
- white glue
- sheet of white paper
- scraps of material, lace and decorative trim

- wiggly eyes (optional)
- cloth or paper tape
- old newspapers

Rinse out can. Wash and dry outside of can. Crush can with hands or stomp with foot to give it an interesting shape. (Aluminum cans are recommended since they crush easily; students can also use cans already bent.)

Cover a well-ventilated work area with newspapers. Paint can black. Let paint dry.

Study shape of can; then paint white facial features on top of can (end with pull-tab top removed). Glue or tape on felt ears, broom straw whiskers and wiggly eyes. Decorate body with braid trim or material scraps if desired. Make tails and antennae with pipe cleaners. Tape in place.

Touch up any mistakes with black enamel paint. When personality is complete, run a bead of glue around bottom of can and set it on top of a tile square or wooden block. (See figure 3-6.)

figure 3-6   *Tin Can Personalities come to life with paint and*
sewing scraps.

Students can type or print a cute or meaningful slogan on white paper and glue it to the tile base, if desired.

teaching tips

Supervise spray painting for safety. Be sure students paint the entire can; they may have to spray twice for good coverage.

Students can look at coloring book pictures or cartoons to learn how to draw and paint facial features.

evaluation

Spray painting; artwork; ingenuity; imagination; and appropriateness of can shape to personality created.

chapter four —

Creating with Crayons

This chapter provides you with a kaleidoscope of craft ideas for students to make. The activities utilize the inexpensive and always close-at-hand materials in unique and unusual ways, allowing students to express their individuality and creativity.

Educational values in this chapter include a sense of color, perspective, design, balance, coordination, manual dexterity and color coordination.

Stained-Glass Window Bookmark

—kaleidoscopic bookmark from crayon chips!

materials

- assorted colors of old crayons (with paper removed)
- potato peeler (or ceramic cleaning tool)
- waxed paper
- 1 sheet of black construction paper
- old newspapers
- electric iron
- scissors
- white glue (or paste)
- ironing board (or sturdy, flat surface)

Cover work area with newspaper. Tear off 2 sheets of waxed paper; cut paper 4″ × 8″. Scrape small crayon chips over 1 sheet of waxed paper. Place second sheet of waxed paper on top. Turn iron to rayon setting.

Cover ironing board (or table top) with several layers of old newspaper. Place prepared waxed paper on board, and cover with 1 sheet of newspaper. Gently glide iron over paper. Iron until chips melt and resemble stained glass. Lift up newspaper to check design; iron until satisfied.

As paper cools, cut 2 window frames from black construction paper. (See figure 4-1a.) Refer to page 28 to enlarge pattern.

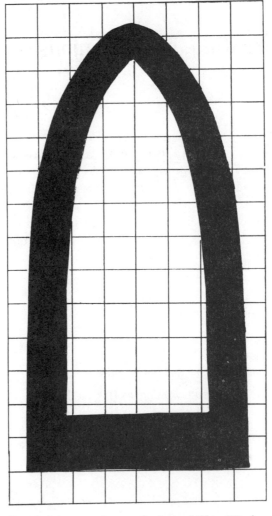

figure 4-1a   *Pattern for Stained-Glass Window Bookmark frame*

Trim cooled wax paper to fit window frame. Glue frame, 1 side at a time, to waxed paper. Let dry.

teaching tips

Small crayon chips work best. Students can crumble large chips between their fingers (or use a rolling pin).

Third- through sixth-graders can iron their own "glass" with supervision. It is advisable to iron designs for younger students.

Make colorful Easter eggs by sprinkling crayon chips on 1 side of egg-shaped paper. Fold paper in half and iron; then open paper and let cool. Students can discover interesting shapes and designs in their eggs.

Chips can also be sprinkled on a 7″ × 9″ sheet of waxed paper picture. Cut a 1″ frame out of black paper and glue on top of cooled picture. (See figure 4-1b.)

evaluation

Use of colors; design; framing; neatness; and originality.

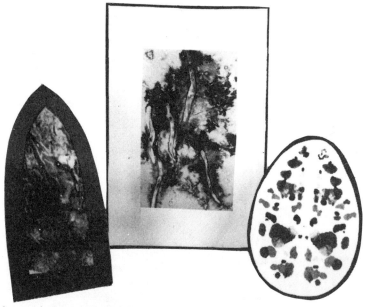

figure 4-1b   *Stained-Glass Window Bookmark—left to right: bookmark, see-thru picture and ornate Easter egg*

Mosaic Mother's Day Vase

—melted crayons transform ordinary bottles into fantastic vases!

materials

• assorted colors of old and broken crayons (with paper removed)

- a paint brush for each color of crayon
- a muffin tin
- old newspapers
- a glass bottle with an unusual shape
- oblong baking dish (big enough for muffin tin to set inside)
- water
- electric hot plate (or make your own—See **teaching tips** section, page 67, for directions.)
- 1 can spray varnish

Cover work area with newspaper. Drop 1 color of broken crayon into each muffin section. Fill the bottom of a baking dish with warm water and set on hot plate. Place muffin tin in pan of water and turn on hot plate. Let crayons melt.

Set muffin tin in center of work area. Keep it in the pan of water to keep melted crayons liquid.

Dip a paint brush in 1 color of melted crayon at a time and dab (or flow) wax on bottle. Work quickly since the wax hardens almost instantly. Use a different paint brush for each color of crayon. Dab (or drip) wax on bottle, alternating colors to create a mosaic effect.

Sprayed cooled, completed vase with clear varnish to brighten and preserve colors. (See figure 4-2.)

figure 4-2   *Mosaic Mother's Day Vase*

teaching tips

Keep wax melted, but not hot during the activity.

Make your own hot plate by placing a 100-watt electric lightbulb underneath a 1-gallon metal can. (Ask the school cafeteria supervisor to save you a can.) Place muffin tin on top of can and plug in light. When wax melts, sit tin in pan of warm water while children paint. If wax cools, reheat on stove.

Kindergarten through second-graders can enjoy this activity with supervision.

Ask students to bring bottles and old crayons from home the day before the activity so no one gets left out.

evaluation

Selection of bottle; use of colors; mosaic design; originality; and overall, completed craft.

Autumn Wood Art

—wood grain adds to the beauty of this art form.

materials

- crayons
- block of wood (any size)
- spray can of clear varnish
- pencil
- black felt-tipped pen (optional)
- old greeting cards
- sandpaper (fine grade)
- tracing paper (optional)
- old newspapers
- hammer
- old rags
- picture hanger (To make hanger, see page 37 for directions.)

Cover work area with newspaper. Set wood block on paper, and sand edges and front. Wipe off dust with an old rag; discard sawdust-covered newspaper.

Use a pencil to sketch (or trace) an autumn picture on front of wood block. (Old greeting cards provide many picture ideas to copy or trace.) Outline picture with new black crayon or black felt-tipped marking pen. Now, color the picture with the grain of wood. Color hard.

When the picture is complete, turn block over and nail a picture hanger on the back near the top. Turn block over. Cover flat surface with newspaper in a well-ventilated area. Spray picture with clear varnish to preserve and brighten colors. (See figure 4-3.)

figure 4-3   *Autumn Wood Art*

teaching tips

Students should select pictures that emphasize the natural grain of the wood. In the illustrated photo, figure 4-3, the tree is drawn on the left side of the block to highlight the knot hole. A light coat of brown crayon further enhances the natural grain.

During the coloring process, students not only discover what a wood grain is, but are delighted with the sensation of coloring wood.

evaluation

Sanding; selection of a picture; use of natural wood grain; coloring; neatness; and originality.

Peek-a-Boo Painting

—black paint makes this picture play peek-a-boo!

materials

- heavy white or light-colored paper
- black liquid tempera paint
- a ½" paint brush
- old tin can (A tunafish can works nicely.)
- bright colored crayons
- old newspapers
- coloring book (optional)
- construction paper (optional)
- tracing paper (optional)
- pencil
- glue (optional)
- scissors (optional)

figure 4-4   *Peek-a-Boo Painting*

Draw a picture on paper. (Young students can trace a coloring book picture.) Outline picture with black crayon; then color picture with crayons. Press hard.

Cover a flat surface with newspaper, and set the picture on newspaper. Pour black paint into a tin can. Dip brush into paint, moving the brush across the picture in long, flowing strokes. Repeat until entire paper is covered. (Paint will not adhere to crayon wax, thus allowing picture to show through.) Let paint dry.

Glue finished picture on a sheet of construction paper, or cut 1"-wide strips of paper and glue around picture for a frame. (See figure 4-4.)

teaching tips

Students must color heavily since a good coat of wax keeps the paint from sticking to the picture. Sometimes students hesitate to smear black paint over their pretty pictures, but once they see what happens and how much fun it is, they will want to make another peek-a-boo painting!

This process creates delightfully spooky Halloween pictures. Draw picture on dark paper, and color design with white crayon. Apply black paint to create an eerie scene scary enough to frighten away witches and goblins!

evaluation

Basic design; coloring; application of paint; originality; and completed activity.

Rainbow Art

—crayon carbon creates a colorful surprise picture!

materials

- 2 sheets of white paper
- crayons
- sharp pencil
- coloring book
- construction paper (optional)
- ruler
- cloth tape or thumb tacks (optional)

Mark ½" lines down one side of a sheet of paper. At each ½" line, draw a crayon line across the paper. Color each space with crayon, alternating colors to achieve a rainbow effect. Press crayons hard. When paper is colored, tear out a picture from a coloring book (or draw a picture).

Place second sheet of white paper on a flat surface. Turn the rainbow-colored piece of paper upside down on top of white paper. Set coloring book picture right side up on top of rainbow paper.

Trace picture with a sharp pencil; press hard. (You can also make pencil marks inside picture for a more solid result. Trace entire picture. Then remove 2 top sheets of paper and view your rainbow art.

Glue finished picture to paper, or cut out picture and paste it inside a plastic meat tray for an instant frame. (See figure 4-5.)

figure 4-5   *Rainbow Art*

teaching tips

Rainbow-colored paper acts like carbon paper. Students must color heavily so the wax carbon will be transferred to the bottom paper.

During pencil tracing, students should not move the papers—it's almost impossible to re-align them once moved. Tape or clip papers together for kindergarten through second-graders.

If you are not sure students have pressed hard enough, let them go over the design again before lifting their carbon paper.

evaluation

Coloring of carbon paper; use of colors; selection of picture; pencil tracing; and originality.

String-Along

—string and crayon combine to create abstract art.

materials

- 2 sheets of white paper
- 1 piece of string 18″ long (Cotton kite string works nicely.)
- crayons

Place 1 sheet of paper on a flat surface. Drop string on top of paper. Spread string out to form loops, curves or a name. Then place the second sheet of paper on top of string design.

Feel position of string with finger tips. From right to left, begin coloring across string. Continue following and coloring over string until entire design has been colored. Tack or tape picture on a wall for everyone to see. (See figure 4-6.)

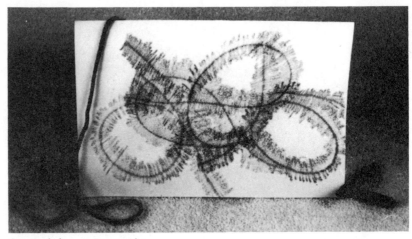

figure 4-6   *String-Along*

teaching tips

This fun craft can be very creative. Students can make their string design all one color or mix colors.

If the first string design is 1 color, carefully lift off top piece of paper and move it in another position. Gently set paper down on top of string design. Color with a different color of crayon. This method can be effectively repeated 3 or 4 times to create an interesting design.

evaluation

Design of string; use of colors; originality; and consistency of coloring pressure.

New Year Calendar

—a classroom craft activity that will be admired and used all year long!

materials

- 3 sheets of 8 × 10 heavy white paper (or 1 poster board)
- 2 sheets of clear, self-adhesive paper 7" wide and 30" long
- pencil
- crayons (or colored pencils or felt-tipped pens)
- calendar for forthcoming year
- old greeting cards, school pictures, and magazine pictures
- scissors
- 14" of colored yarn
- ruler
- black and red ball point pens (or felt-tipped pens)

Cut white paper (or poster board) into 6 cards measuring 4" × 6" each; front and back of cards will be used. (If poster board is used, make sure it is reversible.)

Measure a 3" × 2½" square on both sides of each card. With ruler, mark calendar lines inside small square. Draw lines with a fine-pointed, felt-tipped pen or black ball point pen. Let ink dry.

Write name of month on the top line; write first letter of each day of the week on second line; and begin numbering calendar days on third line. (It is best to draw and complete 1 month at a time since some months have 5 weeks.)

Use an advance calendar to make dates and a red pen to mark special holidays and dates. Decorate each month with colored pictures, magazine or greeting card cut-outs and school pictures.

To avoid confusion, complete January through June calendars; then turn cards over, 1 at a time, and complete July through December. (Take care when turning cards over that flip side is not upside down.)

Draw a July calendar on the back of January; August on February; September on March; October on April; November on May and December on back of June.

figure 4-7   *New Year Calendar—January through June pictured; July through December on back side*

When the calendar months are complete, lay 1 piece of self-adhesive paper on a flat surface. Peel off backing (sticky side of paper will be up).

Lay January calendar on the paper about ¾" from top, leaving ½" of clear paper on each side.

Drop down ½" and stick February on paper. Place remaining 4 months on paper at ½" intervals.

Tie yarn ends together, and stick yarn on paper ½" above the January card. Now, peel paper from back of second sheet of clear adhesive.

Carefully lay sticky side of paper down on top of cards. Begin at top and work down, taking care not to wrinkle adhesive paper. When paper is in place, press around cards and yarn with finger tips to lock in paper. Trim any uneven edges with scissors.

Hang up New Year Calendar by yarn. Flip calendar over at the end of June and continue using. (See figure 4-7.)

teaching tips

Since both sides of the cards are used, double check students to make sure no calendar month is upside down.

Young students will need help measuring and drawing their calendars, as well as applying self-adhesive paper.

If possible, secure small desk calendars from a bank or business. Tear pages apart and glue each month in place; then decorate.

This activity teaches the months of the year, holidays, days of the week, numbers and school events. Encourage children to individualize their calendars noting birthdays, school holidays, and other important or memorable dates.

evaluation

Hand-drawn calendars; artwork; originality; gluing (if any); placement of calendar months on self-adhesive paper; neatness; and overall, completed calendar.

chapter five —

Jiffy Jewelry

What's more fun than making a craft? Wearing it, of course!

This chapter is packed with decorative ideas to adorn the neck, ears and wrist—and they make dandy gifts.

A variety of patterns is provided for the crafts; interchange them with other crafts so students will have more patterns from which to choose.

Educational values in this chapter include imagination, ecology, design, color, proportion, shape, manual dexterity and physical coordination.

Fuzzy Forest Creatures

—furry little pins made from colorful chenille bumps!

materials

- assortment of chenille bumps or fringe balls (found in a craft or fabric store)
- white glue
- felt scraps (assorted colors)
- pin backings (found in craft stores)
- scissors
- medium-sized and large wiggly eyes
- paper punch
- lightweight cardboard (The side of a cereal box works nicely.)
- construction paper (optional)

- pencil (or ball point pen)
- flower centers (found in craft store)
- Ruler

Make basic creature body pattern of lightweight cardboard. (See figure 5-1a.) To enlarge patterns see page 28. Trace pattern on felt and cut out. Lay felt on a flat surface, and glue chenille bumps onto felt. Let glue dry.

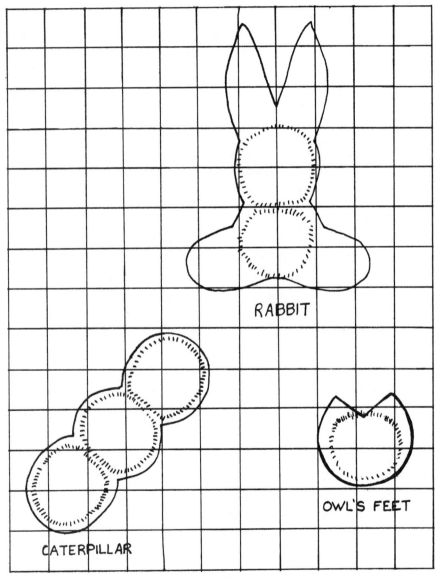

RABBIT

CATERPILLAR

OWL'S FEET

figure 5-1a   *Patterns for Fuzzy Forest Creature*

Glue 2 wiggly eyes on forest rabbit. Cut a paper punched felt circle in half for the rabbit's nose.

Glue 3 bumps onto fuzzy caterpillar shape, and top with 2 medium-sized wiggly eyes. Decorate with felt polka dots made with a paper punch and glue 2 flower-center antennae in place behind eyes.

Little ones will like this wide-awake owl. Cut foot pattern from yellow felt. Glue 1 bump (any color) on felt, and add 2 large, wiggly eyes and a small yellow felt beak.

When fuzzy forest creatures is complete, turn over and glue 1 pin backing in place. Let glue dry. (See figure 5-1b.)

figure 5-1b   *Fuzzy Forest Creatures*

teaching tips

Fourth- through sixth-graders can create their own creature designs. Let them create mice, birds, bears, kitty cats, ladybugs, bumblebees and ducks from chenille bumps.

Boys can pin their forest creates onto their favorite hat or jacket, or they can glue small magnets on the back in place of the pin and stick them on the refrigerator.

To save time, prepare cardboard patterns in advance for young students or pre-cut felt shapes for them.

evaluation

Basic animal body shape (if other than pattern provided); cutting; gluing; facial features; originality; neatness; and overall, completed creature.

St. Patrick's Day Key Ring

—not even a clever leprechaun can hide your keys when they're attached to this fluffy green ball!

materials

- 10 to 12 yards of Kelly green rug yarn
- heavy cardboard or sturdy plastic (The side of a liquid detergent bottle or powdered soap box works nicely.)
- scissors
- pencil
- key ring (found in craft stores)
- tracing paper

Make a key ring pattern of heavy cardboard or sturdy plastic. (See figure 5-2a.) Refer to page 28 for pattern-enlarging directions. Cut out circle.

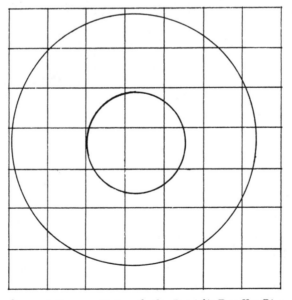

figure 5-2a   *Pattern for St. Patrick's Day Key Ring*

Place yarn end at center of inner circle, and wrap yarn around outside ring of circle. Pull yarn through center hole. (See figure 5-2b.) Continue wrapping until the center hole is filled.

figure 5-2b   *Cardboard pattern of key ring is wrapped with yarn until center hole is filled.*

Use sharp scissors to cut wound yarn along the outside of pattern. With pattern in place, tie a piece of yarn (about 4″ long) around middle of yarn ball. (See figure 5-2c.) Tie yarn tight, make a double knot, and tie on key ring.

Carefully remove pattern. Pop ball on hand (or table) 2 or 3 times to fluff. Trim any uneven edges with scissors. (See figure 5-2d.)

teaching tips

Third- through sixth-grade students can cut their own key ring patterns. Cut out patterns in advance for young students.

Cutting yarn wound around circle is difficult, so give kindergarten, first- and second-graders a helping hand.

Variegated yarn makes a rainbow key ring. Older students can also make key rings in their school colors. Cut 6 yards of yarn in each color. Wind on first color; hold yarn end with finger; secure with second color of yarn and continue wrapping.

Fluffy ball minus key ring can be tied on shoes, hats or roller skates.

evaluation

Basic pattern; winding of yarn; and fullness of completed key ring.

figure 5-2c   *Yarn around cardboard pattern is cut along pattern edge; then yarn is tied together with a 4" piece of yarn. Tie yarn tightly; then tie on key ring attachment.*

figure 5-2d   *Completed key ring, on right, is made by wrapping yarn around cardboard pattern.*

Clip-It-Together Necklace

—paper clips and shiny self-adhesive paper makes this expensive-looking necklace!

materials

- 34 jumbo paper clips
- ⅛ yard colorful metallic self-adhesive paper (Silver looks best.)
- scissors
- ruler
- pencil

Turn self-adhesive paper over. With ruler, measure 34 rectangles 1¼″ wide and 1½″ long; cut out rectangles.

Lay 12 paper clips on a flat surface, and peel backing from 1 rectangle. Lay it sticky side up on the table, and set paper clip on paper. (See figure 5-3a.) Be sure paper clip is centered on paper. Both curved ends should extend evenly beyond paper.

figure 5-3a   *How to cover necklace paper clips: remove self-adhesive paper backing (lower right-hand corner of picture), center clip on paper, sticky side up; fold down one side of paper at a time; overlap joined paper ends and press tightly.*

Fold down 1 side of paper at a time. Overlap joined paper ends, and press tightly. Cover other 11 paper clips.

Now, 1 at a time, slide the small end of the 12 covered paper clips onto 1 uncovered paper clip. Pull clips around to the large end of the paper clip. Cover the paper clip holding the 12 clips.

Next, slip 1 paper clip on the small end of the clip holding the 12 clips, and cover it. Now, add 1 paper clip at a time to top clip, covering as you go until you have added 13 more clips. Join necklace ends with final paper clip slipped through small end of the clip holding original 12 covered clips.

Now, lay necklace on a flat surface. Spread out original 12 clips. Move first 3 clips on each side out of the way. Now, 1 at a time, attach 1 paper clip to the 6 center clips. Cover each paper clip. (See figure 5-3b.)

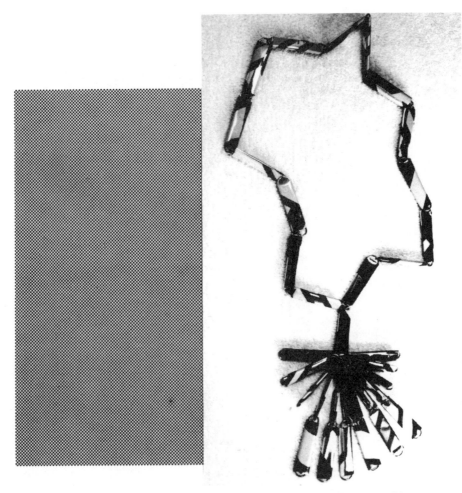

figure 5-3b   *Clip-It-Together Necklace*

Make earrings to match the necklace. Slip 1 large paper clip through small ring of an earring backing, and cover clip with matching paper. For dangling earrings, attach 2 or 3 small paper clips to large clip; then cover.

teaching tips

A short classroom demonstration will aid students with this activity. Care should be taken in drawing and cutting the paper rectangles. Good coverage is essential.

Also, the selection of the self-adhesive paper is important to the success of this craft. The more expensive, metallic-type paper makes the prettiest necklaces.

Paper clips can be spray painted gold (or any other color) before assembly.

After students get the feel of this craft, they can experiment and create different necklace designs. They can also create with smaller paper clips.

evaluation

Cutting of paper; covering; use of color; originality; neatness; and completed necklace.

Swinging Medallions

—shiny, antiqued necklaces are real eye-catchers!

materials

- lightweight cardboard (or poster board)
- scissors
- aluminum foil
- flat black spray paint
- old rags (or paper towels)
- pull-tab rings (from a juice or soft drink can)
- paper punch
- white glue
- plastic jewels (or sequins, small rocks, buttons or shells)
- yarn (or silver chain or key chain)
- newspapers
- pencil
- cookie cutters or stencils (optional)

Draw a design on a piece of lightweight cardboard. (See figure 5-4a.) To

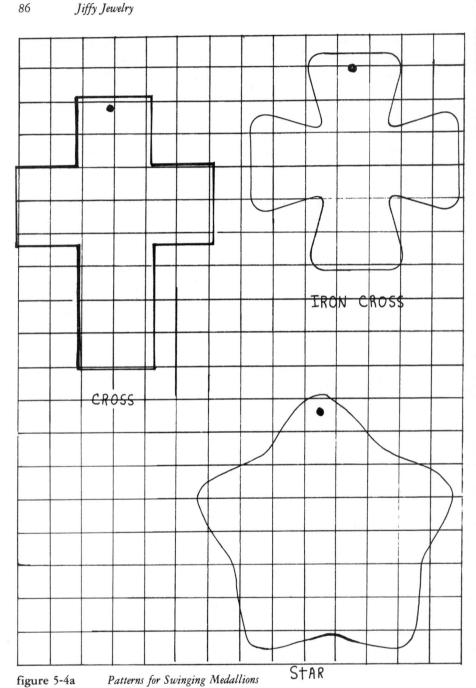

IRON CROSS

CROSS

STAR

figure 5-4a   *Patterns for Swinging Medallions*

enlarge patterns, see page 28. Or, use a stencil, cookie cutter or hand-drawn designs. Cut out cardboard designs. Tear off a sheet of aluminum foil slightly larger than your design. Crinkle foil; then unwrinkle and smooth slightly. Coat cardboard with glue. Place aluminum foil (shiny side up) on glue. Fold edges of foil under cardboard, and scissor trim excess to ¼".

Tear off another piece of foil. Cut exact size of design; crinkle, unwrinkle and smooth. Glue on back of design. Scissor trim any overlapping edges. Let glue dry. Decorate by gluing pull-tab rings (with tab removed) on foil. Let glue dry.

Cover a well-ventilated work area with newspaper. Lay foil-covered design on paper and spray with flat black paint. Immediately wipe off excess paint with an old rag. (The more you wipe, the more shiny the medallion. For a darker look, wipe lightly or respray.) Let paint dry.

Turn medallion over and paint back. When paint dries, glue sequins, beads, buttons, shells, etc. on medallion.

Use paper punch to make a hole in top of medallion. Insert a silver chain or yarn for a necklace or slip on a key ring. (See figure 5-4b.)

figure 5-4b   *Swinging Medallions—necklace and key chain*

teaching tips

Cut young students' patterns in advance, or let them trace cookie cutters. It is also advisable to paint their medallions. They can slip on an old glove and do the wiping.

Antique bracelets are easily made by cutting a strip of cardboard 1" wide and slightly larger than the wrist. (It must be big enough to slip over the hand.) Tape cardboard together, cover with foil, paint and decorate.

By adding string, swinging medallions make attractive wall plaques. Cut design out of heavy cardboard. (The side of a grocery box works nicely.) Pencil sketch in details or facial features. Glue cotton string on pencil lines. (The kind used to fly a kite works best.) This process is much like outlining a mosaic design. Let glue dry.

Tear off a sheet of aluminum foil slightly larger than design; crinkle, unwrinkle and smooth. Glue foil over cardboard and string. Press foil around string areas with fingers (or use a cotton swab); it's not necessary to cover the back. Large designs will require several sheets of foil. Glue overlapped edges together to prevent seams from showing.

When glue is dry, paint design. Quickly wipe off excess paint and let dry. Decorate with beads, buttons, feathers, etc. To hang, tape a soft drink can pull tab on back of the plaque. (See figure 5-4c.)

Coloring book pictures have great design ideas, but keep basic pattern simple for young students.

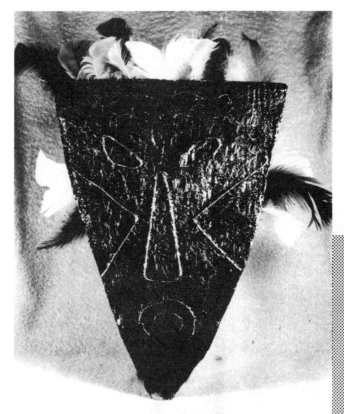

figure 5-4c   *Mask Wall Plaque made from Swinging Medallion—string glued on cardboard, then covered with crinkled aluminum foil dramatizes the finished product.*

Ask students to bring paint and foil and boxes from home to reduce your costs.

evaluation

Medallion—basic design shape; aluminum application; painting; antiquing; decoration; and originality.

Wall plaque—basic design; gluing of string; foil application; painting; decoration; originality; and completed plaque.

Tab Top Flower Pin

—7 rings from soft drink cans and a marble make this clever floral pin!

materials

- 6 pull-tab rings with tabs attached (removed from a soft drink or juice can)
- 1 pull-tab ring with tab removed
- a marble
- scrap piece of felt
- 1 pin clasp
- white glue
- enamel paint (or fingernail polish)

Cut felt scrap into a circle 1½" in circumference. Then 1 at a time, curl all 6 tabs over backward so each tab bends back over the ring. (See figure 5-5a.)

Hold ring without tab in 1 hand. Insert curled tab of another ring through ring in your hand; then insert other 5 rings in this manner. (Curled tab holds 6 rings on seventh ring.)

Apply glue to felt circle, and place joined rings on felt. Space rings evenly to form a circle. Coat ½ of marble with glue. Drop (glued side down) into center of ring tabs. Let dry.

Paint flower petals (ring tabs) with enamel or fingernail polish. If desirable, spray the entire pin with enamel. Do this before gluing marble in place, unless you want marble painted too. When the paint is dry, turn pin over and glue a pin clasp on the back. Let dry. (See figure 5-5b.)

teaching tips

A classroom demonstration will help students quickly create their own flower pins.

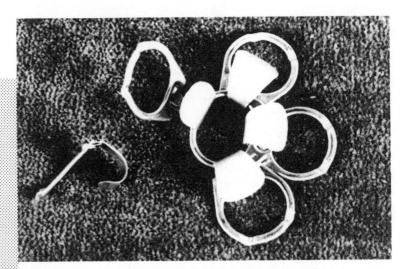

figure 5-5a   *Tab Top Flower Pin—assembly: bent tabs are slipped over one ring (with tab removed) to form basic flower. Joined rings are glued on felt circle and decorated.*

figure 5-5b   *Tab Top Flower Pin—unique necklace or lapel pin*

Flowers can be glued to a coat hanger stem wire for stand-up flowers or attached to a necklace chain.

evaluation

Spacing of pull-tab rings; painting; and originality.

Shrinking Trinkets

—unbelievable foam meat tray jewelry is fun to make, watch and wear!

materials

- plastic foam meat tray (washed and dried)
- scissors
- cookie cutters or stencils (optional)
- felt-tipped marking pens
- paper punch
- aluminum foil
- oven (or portable toaster oven with glass door)
- cookie sheet (or aluminum pie pan)
- ball point pen (with black ink)
- jewelry jump rings (found in craft or hobby store)
- jewelry chain (yarn or string)
- needlenose pliers
- pot holders

Place meat tray on a flat surface. Draw a design or outline a cookie cutter or stencil on meat tray. (See figure 5-6a.) Refer to page 28 for pattern-enlarging directions. Bear in mind that the original design will shrink to about ¼ its size, so don't make the designs too small. (See figure 5-6b.)

Carefully cut out design. Make a hole with paper punch where desired. Color design with felt pen, or outline features with a ball point pen.

Turn oven on medium (325 to 375 degrees). Line a cookie sheet with aluminum foil for regular oven. Set cut-outs in an aluminum pie pan for toaster oven.

Place cut-outs on aluminum about 1″ apart, and set in oven. Watch cut-outs as they swell up, then shrink (approximately 2-4 minutes). Remove from oven, and let cool (approximately 5 minutes).

Attach jump ring in hole and hook to chain or yarn necklace, key ring,

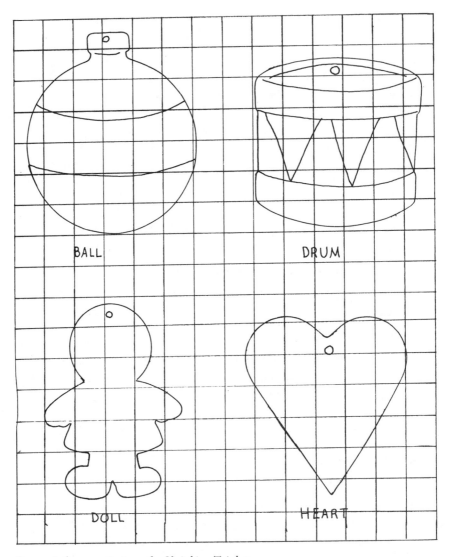

figure 5-6a   *Patterns for Shrinking Trinkets*

earrings or bracelet chain, or glue trinkets without holes to tie tac forms and pin backings. (See figure 5-6c.)

teaching tips

Keep basic cut-out design simple. Complex patterns are difficult to cut and sometimes curl up in the oven.

Oven temperatures vary, so shrink a few experimental trinkets first.

figure 5-6b   *Little girl cookie cutter (left) pattern results in trinket about ¼ the original size.*

figure 5-6c   *Shrinking Trinkets—delightful miniature charms, pins, tie tacs and necklaces*

Some types of meat trays work better than others. Generally, the thicker, more compact types of trays work better than the thin, glossy types.

If oven gets too hot, the cut-outs will curl up as soon as they hit the oven and stick together, ruining the design. If this happens, turn off oven and let it cool; then begin again.

Students will enjoy watching this activity, so try to use a glass-doored oven if possible.

evaluation

Basic design; cutting; coloring or decoration; originality; and completed trinket.

Icy Crystal Jewels

—shimmering crystal clear jewels from plastic pill bottles!

materials

- assortment of empty plastic pill bottles (washed and dried)
- assortment of plastic beads (or sequins, glitter, crayon chips, small stones or shiny pennies)
- cookie sheet (or aluminum pie pan)
- aluminum foil
- oven (or portable toaster oven)
- needlenose pliers
- large jump rings (or fine wire)
- ice pick
- candle
- paper towels
- matches
- pot holders

Cover cookie sheet with aluminum foil. Set pill bottles upright (about 1″ apart) on cookie sheet. (For toaster oven, place bottles in an aluminum pie pan.) Turn oven to 500 degrees (or highest heat).

Drop several plastic beads (or glitter, crayon chips, small stones or a shiny penny) into each bottle. Place tray holding bottles in hot oven. Let bottles melt. (It takes approximately 5 minutes.)

Remove tray from oven. Keep melted jewels on cookie sheet until cool (or lift aluminum foil from tray and set aside to cool). You can also remove jewels from tray with a spatula. Set on aluminum foil or glass to cool. Don't let hot jewels touch each other.

Now, pierce a hole in each jewel. Light a candle and heat the tip of an ice pick over the flame. Push ice pick through the pill bottle. Clean ice pick with a paper towel before making another hole in a different jewel. Blow out candle.

Open a jump ring with pliers and slip through hole. Attach jump ring to a necklace chain, key ring or bracelet. If you don't have jump rings, cut off a small piece of fine wire, push through hole and twist to secure. (See figure 5-7.)

figure 5-7   *Icy Crystal Jewels—small plastic pill bottle (fore-ground) melted to produce crystal jewels. Plastic beads, a penny and a tumbled stone make colorful and unique necklaces and key chains.*

teaching tips

No 2 pieces of jewelry will ever be alike.

Most of the bottles melt in a circular or teardrop shape. Punch hole through the most logical place.

Melted bottles are hot! Let jewels cool at least 10 minutes before touching.

You or an aide should punch ice pick holes in each jewel. Clean ice pick with a paper towel after making each hole to prevent blackening from candle flame.

evaluation

Originality; and completed jewel.

chapter six —

The American Indian

This chapter is a tribute to the history, culture and art form of the American Indian, who played a vital role in the history of our great nation.

While students create, encourage the use of authentic Indian symbols and designs so they can learn about the life-style, habits, beliefs and symbols of our first native Americans.

Educational values in this chapter include the lore of the American Indian, ecology, design, proportion, creativity, spatial relations, manual dexterity and use of color.

Beaded Breechcloth

—braves look authentic in decorative, leather-like breechcloths made from paper bags!

materials

- 1 large paper bag (Each bag makes 2 breechclothes.)
- scissors
- pencil
- ruler
- yarn
- uncooked rice
- assorted colors of food coloring
- 5 or 6 baby food jars (or plastic margarine tubs)
- 5 or 6 plates (or aluminum pie pans or paper towels)

- tracing paper (optional)
- white glue
- old newspapers

Cover work area with newspapers. Color rice. Fill a baby food jar (or margarine tub) ½ full of rice, and add a few drops of food coloring. Screw on lid and shake jar vigorously.

Pour colored rice into a paper plate. Spread out rice and let dry. Dye as many colors of rice as you like.

While rice dries, cut out breechcloth. Lay a folded paper bag on a flat surface.

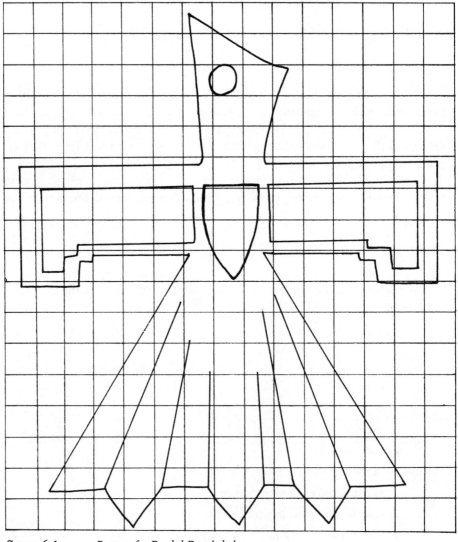

figure 6-1a   *Pattern for Beaded Breechcloth*

Measure and draw a rectangle 11″ wide and 15″ long. Cut out breechcloth. (You will have 2.) Measure up 3″ from the bottom of the breechcloth, and draw a straight line across the 3″ line. With scissors cut a fringe edge to the line. Cut the fringe about 3″ long and ⅛″ wide.

Cut a piece of yarn about 45″ long; turn under 1″ at top (unfringed edge) of breechcloth. Then turn the breechcloth over, and lay yarn inside the 1″ fold line. Tape, staple or glue yarn inside folded paper.

Turn breechcloth back over. Draw an Indian design or symbol on front of breechcloth. (See figure 6-1a.) For pattern-enlarging directions, see page 28. Smear glue on a small section of design at a time. Spread glue with fingertips or a cotton swab.

Press dyed rice into glue, applying 1 color of rice at a time. Pick up breechcloth and shake off excess rice. Glue on another color of rice, and continue until design is complete. Let glue dry.

Indian braves are now ready to tie their breechclothes around their waists. (See figure 6-1b.)

figure 6-1b   *Beaded Breechcloth with Thunderbird design*

teaching tips

Yarn should be long enough to tie breechcloth comfortably around the waist. Students can make 2 breechcloths and have 1 for the back as well as the front. Attach both clothes to 1 string and tie at side.

Increase or decrease size of basic rectangle to fit students.

evaluation

Cutting of breechcloth and fringe; Indian designs; application of colored rice; originality; use of color; and neatness.

Snip-A-Vest

—quick and easy Indian vest from a paper bag!

materials

- 1 large grocery bag
- scissors

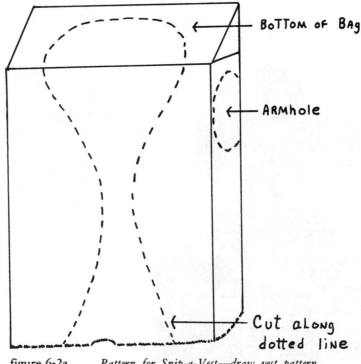

figure 6-2a   *Pattern for Snip-a-Vest—draw vest pattern along dotted line.*

- pencil
- plastic margarine tubs (to wash out brushes and hold paint)
- assorted colors of tempera paint
- paint brushes

Fold bottom of paper bag flat. Lay paper bag, bottom side up, on a flat surface. (The bottom of bag becomes top of vest.) Use a pencil to draw a vest outline on front of the bag. (See figure 6-2a.)

Then cut out vest along pencil lines. (Take care not to cut back of vest.)

Open up bag. Near top of bag vest, draw a large circle on each side for armholes. Cut out circles. Try on vest, and adjust to fit.

Carefully refold bag. With scissors cut a fringe border along bottom and front sides of vest. Fringe strips should be approximately 1″ long and ⅛″ wide. Draw Indian designs and symbols on front and back of vest. (See figures 6-2b and 6-2c.) Paint designs with tempera.

When paint is dry, vest is ready for a classroom play, historical presentation or Indian story.

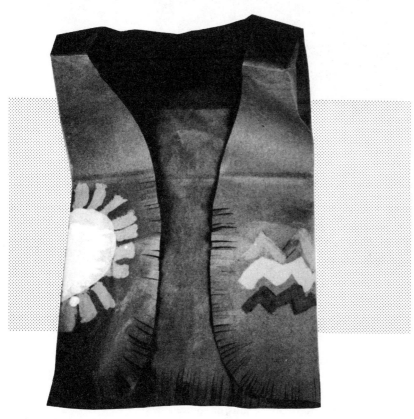

figure 6-2b   *Snip-a-Vest—front view*

figure 6-2c   *Snip-a-Vest—back view*

teaching tips

Ask students to bring paper bags from home. Have a few extra bags on hand just in case someone forgets or cuts wrong.

Vest shoulders can be reinforced with cellophane tape if necessary.

Young students will need help drawing their vests and armholes.

evaluation

Vest design; uniformity of cut fringe; artwork; authenticity of designs and symbols; originality; and neatness.

Painted Desert Pictures

—colorful pictures from tiny grains of colored sand!

materials

- white silica sand, washed, dried and uniformly graded (found in a building supply or craft store)
- assorted colors of permanent ink (optional)
- assorted colors of food coloring
- 5 or 6 clean 1-quart glass jars with lids
- 5 or 6 aluminum pie pans (or sturdy paper plates)
- old newspapers
- large mouth, clear glass jar or bottle (preferably with a glass or cork lid)
- aquarium gravel (optional)
- ice tea spoon
- washable, felt-tipped marking pen (or dark crayon)
- pick-up stick
- cloth measuring tape

First, color the sand. Fill each quart jar ½ full of sand. Pour food coloring into the sand, screw on jar lid and shake vigorously. Add more food coloring until sand becomes desired color.

Pour colored sand into aluminum pie pan to dry. (To speed drying, set pan in sunlight.) Dye as many different colors of sand as you like. Be sure sand is thoroughly dry before making a picture.

[*Note: food-colored sand is ideal for most painted desert pictures. However, the pictures make a colorful, unique base for planted terrariums; and since food coloring is water soluble, sand for terrarium pictures must be dyed with permanent ink. (Ink can be purchased at an art supply store.) Color sand according to food coloring directions.*]

Cover work area with newspapers, and place glass jar or bottle on newspapers. Set pie pans full of colored sand on paper. Now, you are ready to create painted desert pictures.

Wrap a cloth measuring tape around base of glass jar. Divide jar into 8 equal parts. A jar 8″ in circumference will have 8 marks, 1 inch apart. Mark off jar with felt-tipped pen or dark crayon. Remove tape from jar. The marks help keep the sand painting designs uniform and evenly spaced.

Spoon a ½″ layer of sand in bottom of glass container, making sure sand is even. Pour in a second layer of sand. Add sand by placing a spoonful of sand on side of glass and allowing it to flow down sides of jar. When second layer of a different color of sand is in place, you can start to create patterns.

To make a starburst pattern, insert the pick-up stick through top layer of sand at each mark. Push stick into second layer of sand to allow top color of sand to flow into bottom layer. For best results, starburst patterns should be equally

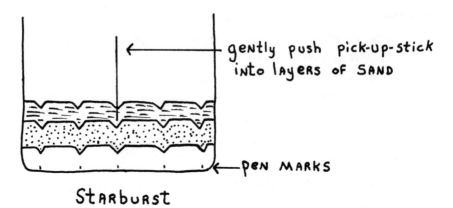

gently push pick-up-stick
into layers of SAND

pen MARKS

Starburst

figure 6-3a   *Painted Desert Pictures—Starburst*

spaced and all the same depth. (See figure 6-3a.) Add as many layers of sand as you like, 1 at a time, creating the starburst pattern in each layer.

To make a triangle pattern, fill bottom of jar with ½″ of sand; then add a second ½″ layer of sand. Use tip of an ice tea spoon to push sand away from sides of glass at each mark. This will create triangles. Pour a layer of contrasting colored sand over triangles for a dramatic effect. (See figure 6-3b.)

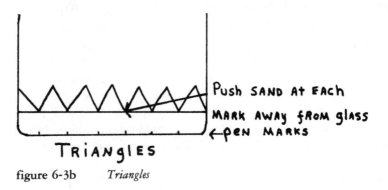

Push SAND At EACh
MARK AWAy fRoM glass
pen MARKS

TRiANglES

figure 6-3b   *Triangles*

To make mountains, seagulls and clouds, fill bottom of jar with green sand. Pour in brown sand, and use ice tea spoon to create mounds in sand. Pour black sand between the mounts to create mountains; then add a little white sand on top of black sand. Pierce white sand with pick-up stick to create a snow-capped, mountain top effect.

Now, pour in blue sand for sky. Make a wavy line (about 1-½″ long) in sand with spoon. Pour a small amount of white sand over wavy line, and add an equal amount of black sand. Now, add a ¼″ thick layer of blue sand. Insert pick-up stick in the center of wavy line and watch a seagull emerge.

Pour white sand in 1 or 2 areas of blue sand. Cover with more blue sand, and white clouds take shape. (See figure 6-3c.)

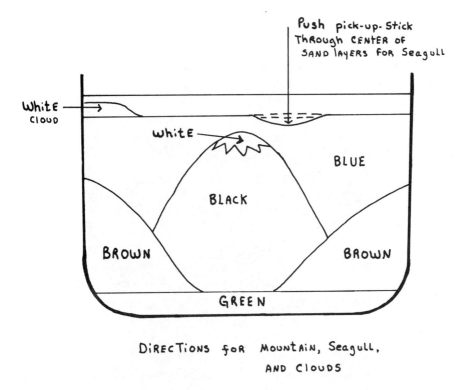

Push pick-up-Stick
Through CENTER oF
SAND layERs FoR SeaguLL

White Cloud

White

BLUE

BLACK

BROWN   BROWN

GREEN

DiRECTioNS foR MouNtAiN, SeaguLL,
AND ClouDS

figure 6-3c   *Mountains, Seagulls and Clouds*

Combine designs provided and make up other designs while creating painted desert pictures. Wash pen or crayon marks off outside of glass. Place lid on completed picture and display proudly. (See figure 6-3d.)

teaching tips

You will see the sand pile up along the sides of glass, and center of jar tends to be void of sand. Fill center with uncolored sand (to save your colored sand) or fill hole with dirt or potting soil if you plan to plant a terrarium.

Students can spoon away their mistakes by pushing sand toward the center.

The selection of the jar is important in this craft. Candy jars, apothecary jars and brandy snifters are ideal. If possible, avoid any design in the glass container itself.

Dyed sand can also be glued like mosaic gravel to designs drawn on poster board, wood or sand paper. Colored sand will keep indefinitely in a cool, dry place.

evaluation

Container used; design; shapes; use of color; originality; and completed craft.

figure 6-3d   *Painted Desert Pictures*

Squaw Headband

—pull-tab rings from soft drink cans make colorful headbands for Indian squaws!

materials

- approximately 20 alike pull-tab rings (from soft drink or juice cans)
- colored plastic tape (at least 2 different colors)
- pencil
- construction paper
- ruler

- plastic drinking straw
- scissors
- paper punch (optional)
- needlenose pliers (optional)

Remove pull tabs from all rings with fingers, or use needlenose pliers. The size of child's head will determine the number of rings required to make each headband. Cut 1 color of tape into 19 strips 2″ long and ½″ wide. Lay 1 strip of tape, sticky side up, on a flat surface.

Place edge of 1 pull ring (where tab was removed) in the center of tape. Ring should be smooth side down on tape. Place edge of second ring against edge of first ring, and wrap tape around both rings to form 1 double ring. Overlap tape edges. (See figure 6-4a.)

figure 6-4a   *Joining of rings to form double ring for Squaw Headband*

Tape 9 more double rings together. Lay in a straight line on a flat surface. Tape curved edges together until you have 1 continuous chain of double rings. Then join final rings with tape. (Test length of headband by placing around head. Increase or decrease the amount of rings until you get a snug fit.)

Cut a different color of tape into long, narrow strips. Wrap them in the center of the first tape strips to decorate headband, or make circles with paper punch and stick on tape.

Draw and cut out paper feather, or use pattern on page 111. Tape a plastic drinking straw to the back and tape to headband. (See figure 6-4b.)

teaching tips

Students can substitute real feathers for paper ones. Rings can be joined with white cloth tape and colored with crayon very economically.

figure 6-4b   *Squaw Headband*

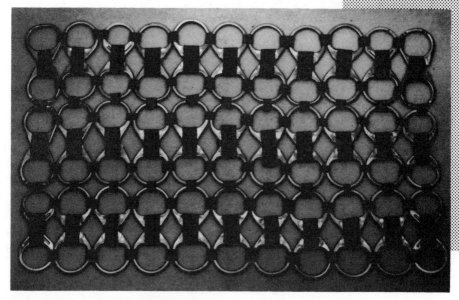

figure 6-4c   *Tab Ring Trivet*

Be sure young students cover joined ring ends completely to prevent the headband from scratching tiny scalps.

Fourth- through sixth-graders can create useful, ornate trivets. (See figure 6-4c.) You will need 66 alike pull-tab rings. Join rings to make 33 double rings. Separate double rings into groups of 11.

Lay 11 double rings on flat surface. Join each inside curved ring with tape. Then join other curved sides of other 2 sets of 11 double rings. Now, lay 1 row of 11 joined rings on flat surface. Place second row directly beneath first row; lay third row beneath second row. Tape curved edges of each row to top row to complete trivet.

Trivets make handy holders for hot and cold dishes and flower pots.

evaluation

Headband—cutting of tape strips; joined edges; use of color; feather; and fit.

Trivet—uniformity of tape strips; use of color; originality; design; neatness; and completed trivet.

Chief's War Bonnet

—everyone can be a chief with this much-feathered bonnet!

materials

- piece of lightweight cardboard (The side of a detergent or cereal box works nicely.)
- construction paper
- pencil
- scissors
- tracing paper (optional)
- 2 6" strips of yarn
- tempera paint (or crayons or felt-tipped pens)
- stapler
- cellophane tape
- 5 plastic drinking straws
- strip of ¼"-wide elastic

Draw basic bonnet design on lightweight cardboard and cut out. (See figure 6-5a.) See page 28 for pattern-enlarging drawings.

Draw and cut out 5 paper feathers. (See figure 6-5b.) Tape a drinking straw

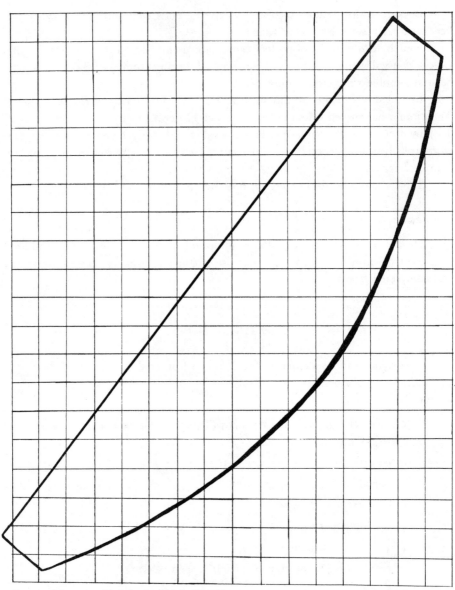

figure 6-5a   *Pattern for Chief's War Bonnet*

to back of each feather. Cut bottom of straws even with feather ends. Draw Indian designs or symbols on front of bonnet. Paint (or color).

Cut a strip of elastic 11″ long (or any length to fit head snugly). Staple 1 elastic end to each side of back of bonnet. Now, staple feathers in place.

Tape each 6-inch strip of yarn to each side of bonnet back; then tape or staple racoon tail or small feather to loose yarn end. War bonnet is now ready for action. (See figure 6-5c.)

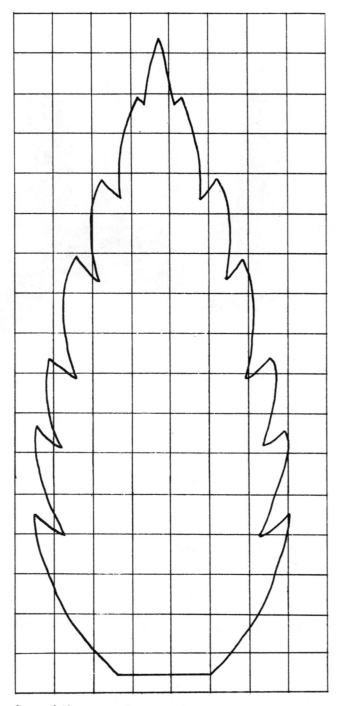

figure 6-5b   *Feather pattern for Chief's War Bonnet*

figure 6-5c   *Chief's War Bonnet*

teaching tips

Students can substitute real feathers for paper ones.

Colored rice left over from Beaded Breechcloths (page 97) can be glued on designs.

evaluation

Cutting of bonnet and feathers; use of color; bonnet decoration; originality; authenticity of designs; and overall bonnet.

Stackable Totem Pole

—cardboard boxes and imagination stack up to create this authentic-looking totem pole.

materials

- assorted shapes and sizes of cardboard boxes (They're yours for the asking at most supermarkets.)

- paper tape
- a large tin can (or plastic pail)
- sand (or dirt or plaster of Paris)
- a tall, straight stick (An old broom stick works nicely.)
- scissors
- soft leaded pencil (or dark crayon)
- sharp knife
- assorted colors of tempera paint
- small and large paint brushes
- old newspapers
- old tin cans (washed and dried with one end removed)

Place stick in center of a large tin can (or plastic pail). Hold stick in place and fill can with sand, dirt or plaster of Paris. (If you use plaster of Paris, let it harden before proceeding.)

Stack cardboard boxes on floor until you are pleased with the arrangement. (Totem pole can only be as tall as your stick.)

When stacking boxes, be sure the bottom box is large enough to cover the tin can or pail holding stick in place. Now, cut a hole slightly larger than stick in center bottom of each box. Push boxes, 1 at a time, down on stick. Be sure all holes are in same place on each box so totem pole will stand up straight.

Tear off rather long strips of paper tape. Tape edges of box sides, fronts and backs together. (See figure 6-6a.)

Draw an owl's beak, bird's wings and buffalo's horns on the sides of extra cardboard boxes. Leave a 6″ square on end of each piece of cardboard for a tab. Make a slit in cardboard box where beak, wings or horns are to be inserted. Insert 6″-square tab into slit in box.

Now, totem pole is ready to paint. For a realistic totem pole, use dark brown or black paint to cover all boxes. Students can paint each box a different color if desired. Let paint dry. (Pour paint into tin cans for easy painting.)

Draw animal and facial features on painted totem pole with soft-leaded pencil or dark crayon. Paint features with tempera. (If you are mixing dry tempera, make paint a little thick to prevent runs.) Use large and small brushes to paint on features. Save a little of each color of paint to touch up mistakes. (See figure 6-6b.)

teaching tips

Bury a fence post in dirt or sand for an outside totem pole. Cut box holes slightly larger than pole and paint boxes with enamel to protect from the elements.

Kindergarten and first-graders can make mini-totem poles by using 2 round cardboard containers, such as the ones potato chips come in. (See figure 6-6c.)

figure 6-6a   *Assembly of Stackable Totem Pole*

Stack 1 can on top of the other, and tape joined ends together. Spray paint cans black or brown, or cover with paper and glue in place.

Draw on animal and facial features, and paint with tempera. Cut bird wings out of construction paper and tape on back of can. Tape real feathers to back of can top if desired.

evaluation

Straightness; painting; facial features; authenticity; and completed totem pole.

figure 6-6b   *Stackable Totem Pole*

figure 6-6c   *Mini-Totem Pole*

chapter seven —

Mother Nature Handicrafts

Mother Nature provides a wealth of craft materials to challenge and delight students. This chapter is designed to stimulate students and to teach them to appreciate, learn, respect and conserve the beauty and creativity of nature.

While many of the crafts utilize natural materials creatively, the end result of others is learning. (It is always wise to contact the proper authority in advance for permission to hike and collect materials.)

Educational values in this chapter include ecology, conservation, design, the 4 seasons, types of fruit bearing trees, types of migratory and other birds, arrangement, proportion, spacial relations, creativity and manual dexterity.

Peanutty Pine Cone Bird Feeder

—a recycled pine cone is a bird's best friend!

materials

- 1 large pine cone
- heavy string (The kind used to wrap parcels works nicely.)
- peanut butter
- beef fat drippings
- uncooked rolled oatmeal
- mixing bowl
- wooden spoon
- table knife
- old newspapers
- measuring cup and spoons

Cover work area with newspapers, and lay pine cone on papers. Tie a long string (length depends upon where bird feeder is to be hung) on stem of pine cone.

Mix 1 cup of peanut butter, ½ cup of oatmeal and 4 tablespoons of fat drippings together. Use a table knife to spread mixture between pine cone scales. Then hang pine cone upside down on a tree branch or other desirable feeding spot.

Hang pine cone where squirrels and cats can't steal it or bother birds during feeding. (See figure 7-1.)

figure 7-1   *Peanutty Pine Cone Bird Feeder*

teaching tips

Weather permitting, make bird feeders outside.

Hang out lots of peanutty feeders in late fall and winter for hungry and migratory birds.

When food is gone, mixture can be reapplied and cone rehung.

Feeders hung near the classroom make ideal bird-watching observatories. Students can keep a sighting chart of "their" birds.

evaluation

Application of mixture to pine cone; location of hung cone; and bird sightings.

Toy Poodles

—miniature French poodles from tree fruits!

materials

- 17 small cone-like fruits from an Australian Pine
- 2 small, wiggly eyes
- 1 tiny black bead (or the black plastic head from a straight pin)
- white glue
- a can of silver or gold spray paint (optional)
- a can of clear, spray varnish (optional)
- sequins
- old newspapers

Assemble fruits, removing the stems from all fruits except 1. Cover work area with newspapers.

Lay 3 fruits on a flat surface, and glue ends together lengthwise; then glue 3 more fruits together lengthwise. Lay joined fruits side by side, and glue joined sides together. (This is poodle's body.)

Now, glue on 4 fruit legs. Glue 1 fruit at each corner of body. Let glue dry.

Turn body over and stand upon legs. Now, glue 3 more fruits together lengthwise. (This is neck and head.) When glue is dry, glue neck and head on top of 1 end of poodle body. Center on joined sides of poodle body.

Glue 1 fruit lengthwise on second top fruit to complete poodle's face. Then glue a small fruit on each side of the second top fruit to make poodle's ears.

Now, glue stem of last fruit on back of poodle between the joined sides of poodle body. (This is the tail.) Let glue dry.

figure 7-2   *Toy Poodles*

Spray poodle with varnish, or paint it gold or silver. Paint in a well-ventilated area. Let paint dry.

Glue 2 wiggly eyes and a black nose on poodle's face. Glue 1 sequin on the very top fruit for a bow. Glue a short strand of strung sequins around poodle's neck for a shiny collar. (See figure 7-2.)

teaching tips

For best results, use all the same size fruits for the poodle except for ears, which should be smaller.

Students can create other animals such as rabbits, bears or giraffes from Australian Pine fruits. Trees producing other small cone-like fruit that make good craft materials are the Horse Chestnut, Sycamore, Gum, Oak, Hickory, Beech and Red Cedar.

evaluation

Selection of fruits; proportion; gluing; design; painting; decoration; originality; and completed poodle.

Forever-Spring Nature Designs

—a beautiful way to preserve spring blossoms and leaves!

materials

- 1 piece of clear self-adhesive paper 7½″ × 10″
- 1 piece of construction paper 8½ × 11″
- dried leaves, ferns and flowers (See drying directions below.)
- glitter (optional)
- dried butterflies and moths (optional)
- old thick telephone directory (or old newspapers)
- 3 large bricks (or a heavy board)
- heavy string (The type used to wrap parcels works nicely.)
- an electric iron (optional)
- wax paper (optional)

First gather dry leaves, ferns and flowers. To dry materials, use the following procedure:

Remove the stems from flowers and leaves so they will lay flat. (Disassemble roses, etc. and later reassemble when dry.) Place items face down on a page near end of telephone directory. Place items close together, but not touching each other.

Turn down ½″ of pages in the directory, and place more leaves and flowers in place. Always leave at least ½″ of space between pages pressing flowers and leaves. When all items are in place, weight down with bricks (or a heavy board). Tie securely with string.

Place directory in a dry, warm place. In about a week, check flowers. Gently rub your finger across a flower; if it's smooth and releases from the paper, it is dry. (See figure 7-3.) If you do not have a thick telephone directory, you can cut up newspapers into 8″ × 10″ sheets. Stack sheets ½″ high. Lay flowers and leaves on top of each stack. Stack together; weight down; and tie securely.

figure 7-3   *Forever-Spring Nature Designs*

When all materials are dried, you are now ready to begin making your Forever-Spring Nature Designs.

Assemble pressed flowers, ferns and leaves. Lay construction paper on a flat surface, and arrange a design on construction paper. When you are pleased with the design, pull backing off the self-adhesive paper. Lay paper sticky side up on a flat surface. Then 1 at a time, lay pressed items right side down on sticky paper; then complete design. Sprinkle a little glitter on design, or add a dried butterfly or moth for effect.

When design is complete, pick up self-adhesive paper and lay it sticky side down on piece of construction paper. Center design on construction paper, leaving a 1″ border all around the sides. Press self-adhesive paper with fingertips to secure it to construction paper.

To make picture more sturdy, glue construction paper to a piece of equal-sized cardboard. Tape an expanded paper clip (or pull-tab ring from a soft drink can) to the back of picture for a hanger.

teaching tips

The materials must be dry before pressing. Moisture will turn them brown. Also, be sure the directory (or stacks of newspaper sheets) is weighted down and tied well. Air spaces between the pages will wrinkle and fade the flowers and leaves.

If you are in a hurry to make nature designs, place leaves and flowers on stack of newspaper. Cover with wax paper, and press with a hot iron.

Remember, all designs must be laid upside down on sticky side of paper. Take care when overlapping items. If you remove the design, item by item, from the construction paper, it will be exactly as you want it to appear.

Self-adhesive designs can also be stuck onto another equal-sized piece of adhesive paper or a piece of wood.

evaluation

Drying: flatness and color of dried flowers, leaves and ferns.

Assembling: nature design; use of color; imagination; placement of items on self-adhesive paper; application of design to construction paper; and completed craft.

Idle Finger Art

—fingers make "thumb" fun art!

materials

- assorted colors of food coloring
- ball point pen (or fine felt-tipped pens)
- cosmetic cotton squares
- paper towels
- plastic coffee can lids
- construction paper
- inked stamp pads (optional)

- old newspapers
- soap and water

Cover work area with newspapers. Place 1 cosmetic cotton square in each plastic coffee can lid; then set each lid on a paper towel. Saturate cotton with 1 color of food coloring. Fill as many lids as you like with different colors of food coloring. (You can use pre-inked stamp pads instead of cotton squares, but make sure ink is washable.)

Place a piece of construction paper on newspaper. Press 1 finger or thumb into food coloring. Gently wipe excess food coloring off on paper towel. Now, press finger on construction paper to form a print. Let food coloring dry. Use a ball point or felt-tipped pen to draw details on fingerprint.

Create fat, green frogs; bluebirds; red ladybugs; gray mice; green trees; crazy caterpillars; blue pussy willows; butterflies and owls sitting on a drawn tree branch. (See figure 7-4.)

figure 7-4   *Idle Finger Art*

Dip only 1 finger in each color to prevent colors from blending, or wash hands before dipping the same finger into a different color of paint.

When craft is complete, roll up newspapers and discard.

teaching tips

Stamp prints on the inside of a shoe box lid for already framed pictures. Tape a paper clip hanger on back. Paint printed picture background with felt-tipped pens or food coloring, using a cotton swab as a brush.

Idle finger art is a clever way to decorate gift stationery and note cards—and they make cute greeting cards!

evaluation

Creativity; use of color; artwork; sharpness of prints; originality; and completed prints.

Autumn Leaf Prints

—you'll never believe it until you try it!

materials

- any color poster board
- assorted colors of powdered tempera paint
- several teaspoons
- several tea strainers (or flour sifters)
- old newspapers
- solid vegetable food shortening
- paper towels
- can of clear spray varnish
- soap and water
- collection of freshly cut leaves and flowers (Select some that are sturdy and have good veins and interesting shapes.)

Cover a flat surface with newspapers. Cut poster board into desired shape or size; then lay shiny, smooth side of poster board on a flat surface covered with newspaper. (Use only shiny, smooth side of poster board; otherwise, excess paint will stick to surface and ruin design.)

Lay leaves and flowers on newspaper. Dip a paper towel into food shortening, and wipe shortening on leaf or flower. Good coverage is essential for a good print; however, it is not good to overgrease leaf or flower. (Check back of the leaf before applying grease. Many times the back has better veins than the front.)

Carefully lay shortening-coated side of leaf down on poster board. With a clean paper towel smooth out leaf, transferring shortening to poster board. (Take care not to move leaf in this position.) Carefully lift leaf off the poster board, and place it on newspaper. (You will be able to see a faint outline of leaf on poster board.)

Let print rest for a minute. Now, dump 2 or 3 heaping teaspoons of dry, powdered tempera paint into a tea strainer. Hold strainer over the leaf print and shake gently. Sprinkle paint over the entire print.

Wait 1 minute. Now pick up top of poster board and gently tap bottom of board on table. The excess paint will fall off on the newspaper. Set picture in clean, safe place for 10 or 15 minutes.

Pick up newspaper where you painted, and pour excess paint back into strainer for another picture. (Use a different teaspoon and strainer for each color of paint.) Wash and dry hands.

In a well-ventilated area, covered with newspapers, spray varnish on picture. Let varnish dry. (See figure 7-5.)

figure 7-5   *Autumn Leaf Prints*

teaching tips

A good leaf gently handled will make numerous prints. Recoat with shortening before each use.

Autumn leaves out of season? Coat students' hands with shortening, and press hands on white poster board. Sprinkle on black paint for dramatic results.

Take care not to smear prints before varnishing. Even varnished prints should be handled carefully.

Students can bring leaves and flowers from home or gather material on a classroom field trip.

evaluation

Selection of leaf or flower; use of color; design; originality; paint coverage; and completed print.

Year 'Round Terrarium

—clear plastic drinking cups are transformed into miniature gardens!

materials

- 2 alike clear plastic drinking cups
- aquarium gravel (any color)
- rich soil
- tiny plants
- moss (optional)
- small figurine (optional)
- cellophane tape
- old newspapers
- a tablespoon
- water

Weather permitting, this is a nice outdoor activity. If working inside, cover work area with newspapers.

Set plastic cups on the paper, and place 1 tablespoon full of aquarium gravel in bottom of 1 cup. Fill remainder of cup almost full with rich soil.

Plant 1 or 2 tiny plants in soil, and place moss around plants if desired. Sprinkle a little aquarium gravel on top of soil or moss. Set a small figurine in soil. Then sprinkle about 1 tablespoon full of water over plants.

Pick up second plastic cup. Turn it upside down and set on top of planted cup. Tear off a strip of cellophane tape long enough to go around the joined ends of the cups. Then press tape around both cup edges to unite. Set terrarium in minimum sunlight. (See figure 7-6.)

teaching tips

Any size plastic drinking cups will work as long as they are identical. Tape a pretty bow on top of terrariums for gifts to persons in hospitals or nursing homes.

A field trip will reap a bounty of plants and soil. Students can bring their own

figure 7-6   *Year 'Round Terrarium*

figurines from home or make their own classroom critters, such as those on page 23.

Sealed terrariums will create their own moisture and seldom, if ever, need watering.

evaluation

Proportion of plants and figurine to terrarium size; originality; creativity; and completed terrarium.

chapter eight —

Puppet Pageantry

The activities in this chapter have been limited to puppet ideas that students can make in the average classroom. No sewing is required, so even the youngest student can create every puppet.

Because their appeal is so magical, puppets are superb educational tools, deriving benefits such as ingenuity; physical and manual dexterity; reading and/or relating; coordination; self-confidence; public speaking and listening as well as knowledge reaped from the puppet show dialogue.

Rainy Day Finger Puppets

—your fingers make the puppets do the walking!

materials

- cellophane tape (or stapler)
- construction paper
- scissors
- pencil
- crayons (or felt-tipped pens)
- buttons, material and lace scraps (optional)
- glove (optional)
- tracing paper (optional)

Enlarge and cut out basic puppet body on construction paper. (See figure 8-1a.) To enlarge pattern, see page 28.

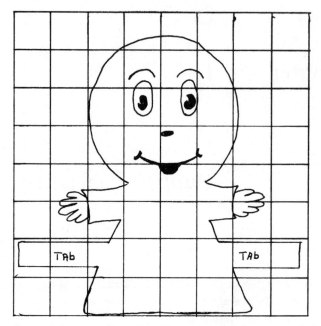

figure 8-1a   *Rainy Day Finger Puppets—basic puppet body*

figure 8-1b   *Rainy Day Finger Puppets*

Draw and color facial features and dress (or clothing) on puppet body. (Or you can glue on fabric dresses, lace trim and button eyes.) Pull side tabs behind puppet back, and tape or staple ends together.

To give puppet legs, slip index and third fingers through joined tabs; adjust width of tabs until puppet fits comfortably. (See figure 8-1b.)

teaching tips

Make puppet's legs and feet more realistic and rest of hand less visible during play by cutting 2 fingers from an old glove. Slip glove on hand, placing 2 uncovered fingers inside puppet tabs.

Students can make an entire family of puppets. Other puppet bodies can be made by tracing cookie cutters or borrowing ideas from coloring book pictures.

Another cute rainy day finger puppet is an elephant with a finger for its trunk. (See figure 8-1c.) Enlarge pattern according to directions on page 28.

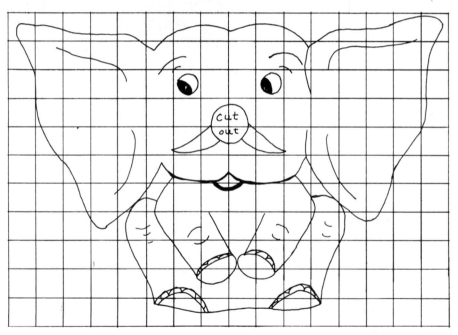

figure 8-1c   *Pattern for Elephant Puppet*

Draw and color facial and body features before cutting out elephant. Then insert a finger through hole to make elephant's trunk come alive. (See figure 8-1d.)

evaluation

Basic puppet design; artwork; proportion; neatness; originality; and completed puppets.

figure 8-1d   *Elephant Rainy Day Finger Puppet*

Leapin' Leprechauns

—mystical Irish elves make high-jumping puppets!

materials

- tongue depressor (or small stick)
- cellophane tape (or white glue)
- construction paper
- crayons (or felt-tipped pens)
- scissors
- pencil
- tracing paper (optional)

Make a paper Leapin' Leprechaun pattern. (See figure 8-2a.) Refer to page 28 for enlarging techniques. Draw and color facial features and body. Cut out puppet. Glue (or tape) stick to back, lower bottom of puppet.

Now the leprechaun is ready to leap over a giant mushroom, pot of gold or right off the stage! (See figure 8-2b.)

figure 8-2a   *Pattern for Leapin' Leprechaun*

teaching tips

Stick puppets are very versatile and easy to hold and manipulate. Students can also make other puppets using other patterns.(See figure 8-2c.)

For example, students can cut out characters from old greeting cards or foam

figure 8-2b　　　*Leapin' Leprechaun*

DUCK

figure 8-2c　　　*Other puppet patterns*

Soldier

Ghost

figure 8-2c (*continued*)

meat trays and glue them on a stick. (See figure 8-2d.) Draw and cut out a meat tray design. (See figure 8-2e.) To enlarge pattern, see page 28. Use scissor tip or pencil point to etch design in foam, then color puppet with felt-tipped pens (or crayons) and tape stick on back.

The wooden tongue depressor itself can be a puppet, too. Draw facial features and glue on material clothing. Wooden puppets make dandy, handy bookmarks.

figure 8-2d   *Foam Meat Tray Puppet*

evaluation

Drawing; cutting; originality; coloring; decoration; imagination; and completed puppets.

figure 8-2e   *Pattern for Meat Tray Puppet*

Carton Critters

—finger fun from egg carton sections!

materials

- plastic egg carton
- construction paper

- small, wiggly eyes (or buttons)
- glitter
- white glue
- lace scraps
- felt-tipped pens (kind that write on anything)
- scissors
- ball point pen (optional)
- tracing paper (optional)

Draw or trace puppet pattern on construction paper. (See figure 8-3a.) To enlarge, see page 28.

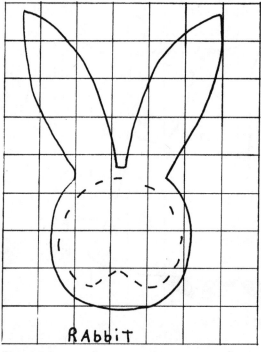

RAbbit

figure 8-3a   *Basic patterns for Carton Critters*

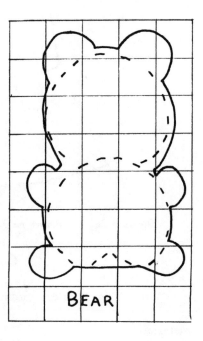

BEAR

GluE Cut Egg SEctioNS

oN doTTED LiNES

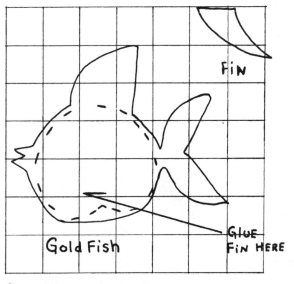

figure 8-3a   *(continued)*

Cut out construction paper pattern; then cut out sections from bottom of an egg carton. Trim each egg section with scissors, cutting away excess until each section measures approximately 1" and ⅝" in circumference.

Cut a "V" shape about ½" wide and ½" deep in bottom of each egg section (or any size large enough to allow a finger to slip through). Smear glue around the outside edge of egg section, and set glued side of section down on paper pattern. (Be sure finger hole is at bottom of pattern.) Let glue dry.

figure 8-3b   *Carton Critters—left to right: fish, rabbit, pig*

Decorate puppet. Glue 1 wiggly eye on goldfish; glue pectoral fin in place and sprinkle gold glitter on egg section and paper pattern. Adorn rabbit with black paper whiskers, red paper mouth, pink paper ears and wiggly eyes. (See figure 8-3b.) The bear gets a lace bow tie, black paper nose, wiggly eyes and hand-drawn mouth. (See figure 8-3c.)

Slip 1 finger through hole in bottom for storytelling.

figure 8-3c   *Carton Critter Bear*

teaching tips

Make sample patterns from lightweight cardboard for young students. Be ready to help them cut out egg sections.

Plastic cartons in which quick-service restaurants serve hamburgers make cute puppets like Freddy Frog. (See figure 8-3d.)

Freddy's mouth is the front of the carton with upper tab cut off. His eyes are 2 joined sections of a plastic egg carton glued in place. Wiggly eyes are glued in center of each section, and construction paper eyelashes are taped in place. Add 4 black, paper webbed feet, and Freddy looks ready to hop. His pink body is covered with glued-on black paper spots.

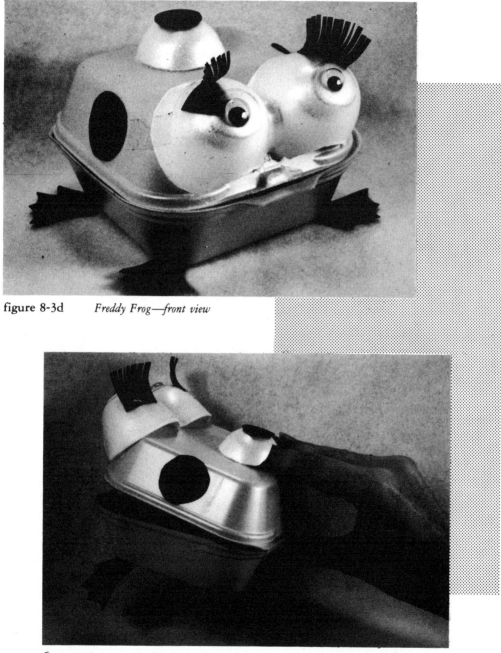

figure 8-3d   *Freddy Frog—front view*

figure 8-3e   *Freddy Frog—back view*

A large wart on top of his back is made from 1 carton section cut exactly like those used to make finger carton critters. Glue the "V" cut to the back so you can slip in a finger. On back bottom of carton, glue a strip of paper in place. Leave it loose so you can slip in your thumb. (See figure 8-3e.)

Tape a long, red paper tongue inside Freddy's mouth. Open and shut his mouth by manipulating thumb and finger inserted in paper strip and upper wart.

evaluation

All puppets on their originality; artwork; proportion; audience appeal; and neatness.

Foam Ball Puppets

—professional-looking puppets make storytelling fun!

materials

- small, round and egg-shaped foam balls (found in craft supply and variety stores)
- tempera paint
- paint brushes
- clay (or paper cups filled with sand)
- old newspapers
- scraps of yarn, lace and ribbon
- material and felt scraps
- buttons, fringe balls and sequins
- wiggly eyes
- pipe cleaners
- plastic-headed straight pins
- paper nut cup
- pencil
- spoon
- white glue
- wooden toothpicks
- popsicle stick
- colored feathers

Assemble all required materials. Cover work area with newspapers. There are several types of foam ball puppets presented here, or invent your own characters.

To make a big-nosed clown or dutch girl puppet, use a spoon to scrape out a hole in foam ball. Make it large enough to slip third finger into. (See figure 8-4a.)

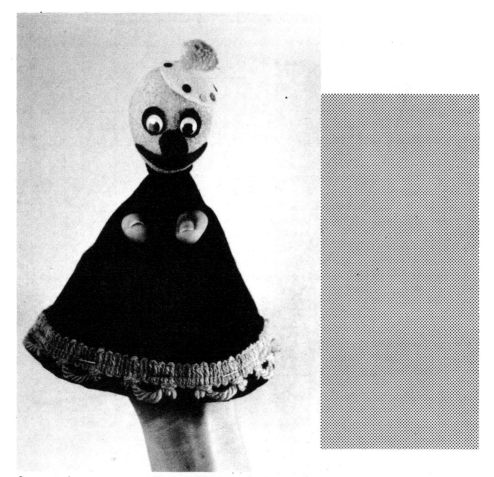

figure 8-4a   *Foam Ball Puppets—Big-Nosed Clown with
cone-shaped felt dress*

Then, stick ball on a pencil to paint with tempera. Let paint dry. (You can save time and spray paint balls, but be sure and use paint recommended for foam or the balls will dissolve.)

Set painted ball in a glob of clay (or paper cup filled with sand) until dry.

Cut out clown or dutch girl dress. Make big-nosed clown's cone-shaped dress out of felt. (See figure 8-4b.) For pattern-enlarging techniques, see page 28.

Cut out dress, make the center, then lay flat. Measure 1″ on either side of center mark. Measure down 2″ from 1″-marks, and draw a small circle on each side of dress. Circles should be about ½″ in circumference or any size large enough to slip the index and fourth finger through. Then cut out circles.

Decorate front of dress with lace, rick-rack or braid. Glue or staple trim in place.

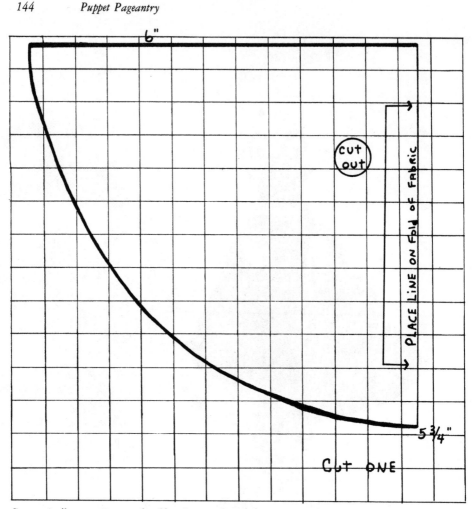

figure 8-4b   *Pattern for Clown's cone-shaped dress*

Lay felt right side down on flat surface. Fold 1 side edge down center back line, and run a bead of glue down outside edge of felt. Fold opposite side edge of felt over. Place on top of glue, and let dry.

To make dutch girl's fabric dress, enlarge basic clown dress pattern to a full circle. (See figure 8-4c.) Cut out 2 finger holes for arms and cut a third hole in the very center of the circle for third finger, which will support the head. Decorate as desired.

Now, complete puppet head. Glue wiggly eyes, fringe ball nose and red, felt mouth on 1 ball for a clown. Top with a felt circle hat (glued together at side edges) adorned with sequins and a fringe ball pompon.

Glue wiggly eyes and a fancy button mouth on dutch girl head. Glue yarn pieces on top for hair. Run a bead around inside edges of paper nut cup, and sit on top of hair. Insert plastic flower through bottom of nut cup hat.

figure 8-4c   *Dutch Girl with material circle dress*

Assemble hand puppets by placing the dress on 1 hand. Slip proper fingers through arm holes, pushing third finger through center hole. Stick on puppet head. (Young students can eliminate holes and push a long stick up through the center of the dress into the puppet head. If the head falls off, dab some glue on dress and then push into head.)

Make a hot pink mouse puppet-on-a-stick by inserting a stick into center bottom of an egg-shaped foam ball. (See figure 8-4d.) Paint the ball pink. Cut 2 ears, a nose and 2 feet out of black felt. (See figure 8-4e.) To enlarge patterns, see page 28.

Glue large wiggly eyes on largest end of the dry ball. Cut and glue broom-straw whiskers under the eyes. Top with a black felt nose.

Apply glue to narrow edges of mouse ears. Then lay a straight pin in the center of each ear and fold felt around the pin. (The sharp point of the pin should stick out below the bottom of the ear.) When glue dries, stick ears in place on mouse head.

Curl the tip of a long, pink pipe cleaner; stick into back of ball for a tail. Tape

figure 8-4d   *Mouse Puppet-on-a-Stick*

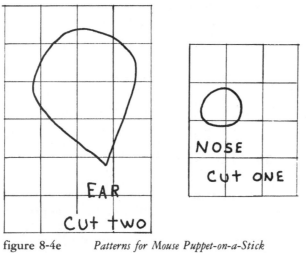
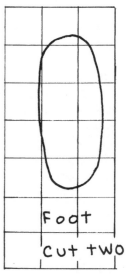

figure 8-4e   *Patterns for Mouse Puppet-on-a-Stick*

(or glue) ½ of a wooden toothpick to the underside of each felt foot. Use straight pins to adhere feet to foam ball. Hold stick in 1 hand and make the puppet move.

teaching tips

A great variety of puppets can be made from foam balls. Students can create snowmen, Easter rabbits, Santa Claus, feathered birds and many other holiday and storybook characters.

Ask students to bring fabric scraps and other items from home to share.

For a class presentation, students can make a puppet for each main character in a story to be enacted. Each student can operate his or her own puppet.

evaluation

Creativity; originality; imagination; neatness; appeal of facial expressions; and completed puppets.

Hold 'Em-Up Puppets

—giant puppets for king-sized shows!

materials

- heavy construction paper (or lightweight cardboard)
- pencil
- scissors
- crayons
- cellophane tape
- greeting cards and coloring books (optional)

Draw a figure on a piece of paper. (Puppet in photograph is 12" high and 10" wide at the widest point.) Outline puppet features with a dark crayon. Then color puppet and cut out. (See figure 8-5a.)

Cut out a long, narrow strip of paper. (One in photograph, figure 8-5b, measures 1½" wide and 7" long.) Tape paper strip handle to back of puppet. (See figure 8-5b.) Tape strip loose so hand can slip through and hold and manipulate puppet.

teaching tips

Students can get puppet ideas from greeting cards and coloring books. Make puppets as large as you like, even life-size! (For very large puppets, make them from sides of cardboard boxes, such as those washing machines or furniture come in.)

figure 8-5a   *Hold 'Em-Up Puppets*

figure 8-5b   *Paper holding strip of Hold 'Em-Up Puppet*

Cut out cardboard puppet with a kitchen knife. Paint life-size puppet with tempera, and staple 2 paper strips on the back of the puppet to hold and manipulate.

Giant puppets are ideal for out-of-doors presentations. And, they are good for shows with a large audience because they can be seen easily.

evaluation

Puppet shape; artwork; cutting; originality; and completed puppet.

Mini- and Maxi- Theaters

—cardboard boxes are transformed into perfect puppet theaters!

materials for mini-theater

- 1 large, round oatmeal box with lid
- self-adhesive paper (optional)
- wrapping paper (tempera paint or a comic page from a newspaper)
- paint brush (optional)
- glue
- large button
- string
- scissors
- old magazines
- construction paper
- kitchen knife (optional)
- pencil
- ruler
- cellophane tape (optional)
- compass point

Lay oatmeal box on its side. Measure down 2″ from the top, and draw a 5″ line across the 2″ line. Draw a 5″ line down each side of box at each end of horizontal, 5″ line.

Then draw a second vertical 5″ line across bottom of box. (This forms the stage opening.)

Cut out 5″ square with a knife or scissors. Lay wrapping paper (or comic page) on a table. Cut paper the proper width and length to cover box sides, leaving a ½″ excess at top and bottom. Glue paper to box. Glue excess ½″ over box ends. Cut 2 circles of paper slightly smaller than the box ends, and glue 1 circle on each end of the box. (You can cover box with self-adhesive paper or paint it with tempera. Let paint dry before proceeding.)

Cut away paper covering the 5″ square stage opening. Leave at least ½″ excess on all sides to fold back and glue inside opening. (Cellophane tape will help hold paper in place while glue dries.)

Cut curtains and a valance out of paper. Glue or tape inside the stage opening.

Find a background picture in a magazine. Cut out and glue inside box directly behind the stage opening. Punch a hole in center top of box with a compass point, and push an 8″ piece of string halfway through the hole. Tie a button to top end of string. Then tape or tie a puppet on string end inside box.

Operate puppet by pulling string up and letting it slide back down through the hole. (See· figure 8-6a.) See page 133 for puppet ideas. (Replace stick with string.)

figure 8-6a   *Mini-Theater from oatmeal box*

teaching tips

Students can cut a piece of scrap material (or carpet) to fit inside the box bottom for a stage floor.

evaluation

Covering of box outside; stage background; theater decoration (if any); originality; and proportion of puppets to theater size.

materials for maxi-theater

- refrigerator shipping carton (available at an appliance store or a warehouse)
- knife
- pencil (or dark crayon)
- old shower curtain
- shower curtain hanging hooks
- broomstick (with broom sawed off)
- paint (enamel or tempera)
- paint brushes
- old tin cans (to hold paint)
- old newspapers

Draw and cut a door in back of box. (See figure 8-6b.) (The door will be almost as large as the box back.) On each side of box near the top, cut a hole slightly larger than broomstick end.

Draw and cut out a window type opening for stage on box front. The size will depend upon the box and height of your students. (See figure 8-6c.)

Cover work area with newspaper. Paint front and sides of box; then decorate front with flowers or storybook characters.

Attach hanging hooks to shower curtain. Slide hooks on broomstick, and insert broomstick ends through holes in top box sides. Upon entering the theater, pull curtain backdrop across door opening.

teaching tips

For a professional little theater, try covering the box with red brick, self-adhesive (or crepe) paper.

Fourth- through sixth-graders can create a theater that can be used for many years. Cut out box openings in advance for young students. They will enjoy painting their theater, perhaps outside on a nice day. (The theater also makes a terrific play store or house for kindergarten and first-grade students.)

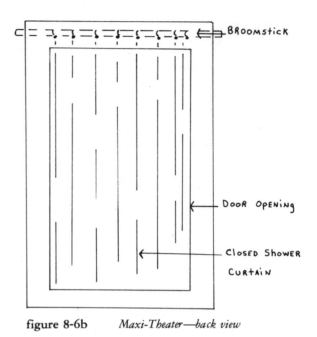

figure 8-6b   *Maxi-Theater—back view*

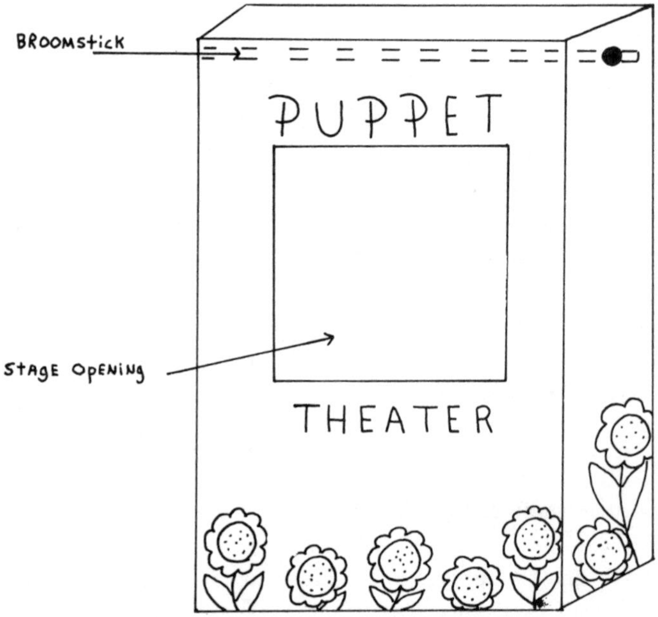

figure 8-6c   *Maxi-Theater—front view*

Other puppet stage ideas may also be used to create ready-made stages that require less time and preparation. For example, an instant stage can be set up by turning a rectangular table on its side. Students can work from behind the table. Or, set 2 chairs back to back about 3 feet apart. Set a broomstick on top of chair backs, and thumbtack a sheet or piece of oil cloth to broomstick. (See figure 8-6d.)

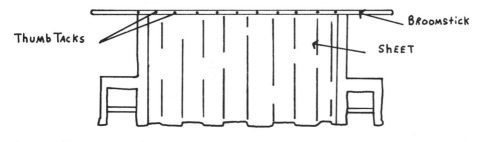

figure 8-6d   *Chair-Sheet Stage*

If possible, place chair or table stage in front of a blank wall or blackboard to eliminate any distractions.

evaluation

Stage size in relation to box size; painting and decoration of theater; neatness; originality; and completed theater.

chapter nine —

Gift Creations

Children love to make surprises for their parents and friends, and this chapter offers you a variety of gift ideas for all seasons and occasions.

Gift Creations is a lesson in sharing, and each activity produces an attractive decorative or useful item. Children not only have the pleasure of making something for someone else, but strive to do their best since the gift is for someone they love.

Educational values in this chapter include manual dexterity through cutting, shapes and sizes, perception, colors and design.

All-Occasion Block Plaques

—cheerful wooden plaques make sensational give-aways!

materials

- scrap block of wood (ideal size 6½″ × 7½″ × 1″ thick)
- white glue
- assortment of used greeting cards (with backs removed)
- 1 bone ring (kind used to hang cafe curtains)
- ribbon scraps
- ¼″ paint brush
- newspaper
- stapler
- damp cloth
- sandpaper (coarse and fine grain)

Spread newspaper over work area. Sand 4 edges, back and front of wood until smooth. Wipe wood with damp cloth to remove any trace of sawdust, or you'll have a bumpy finish. Throw away paper used in sanding and cover area with clean paper.

Select a greeting card to suit the season or occasion, and cut picture to desired shape and size. Picture should be smaller than wood block, leaving a border to act as a frame.

Apply coat of glue to front and sides of wood. Let glue set until tacky. Then press picture in place. Smooth out any air pockets with finger tips. Let glue dry. (See figures 9-1a and 9-1b.)

figure 9-1a   *All-Occasion Block Plaques—Christmas,*
Fourth of July, anytime!

Brush on second coat of glue, and let dry. A third coat can be applied if desired. (If glue is too thick to spread evenly, thin with few drops of water.)

Let plaque dry overnight; then prepare hanger. (See Ribbon Hang-up, page 37 for directions.)

teaching tips

Pour glue into muffin tin (or plastic egg carton) for easy application. Wash brushes immediately after use.

Students can make 3 or 4 small pictures and join together by stapling each plaque, evenly spaced, to 1 long strand of ribbon.

figure 9-1b   *All-Occasion Block Plaques—Wooden Valentine*

Perky plaques have a natural wood frame; but if colored background is desired, sand wood, then brush or spray with quick-drying enamel or acrylic paint. Let paint dry. Apply glue according to directions on page 156; then follow remaining directions in that section.

evaluation

Size, shape and design of picture selection in relation to theme of activity and wood block; general workmanship; and completed plaque.

Jack Frost's Soap Art

—icy wax frosting makes picturesque soap almost too pretty to use!

materials

- assorted used greeting cards (winter scenes)
- rick-rack (thin braid or lace trim)
- ½" paint brush
- new bar of soap (with wrapper removed)
- paraffin wax (kind used to make candles or used in preserving)
- sterno can
- matches
- base of fondue dish
- empty tin can (with label removed)
- scissors
- white glue
- newspapers
- glitter (optional)

Select a greeting card picture, and cut to fit inside bar of soap, leaving equal border around all sides. Spread small amount of glue on back of picture, and center on soap. Picture should lay flat. [*Note: some bars of soap have a lot of writing on them. Select a bar with the least amount of printing. Picture will cover writing. Other soap has raised printing, which can be scraped away with the edge of a spoon.*]

After picture is in place, apply glue to underside of rick-rack (braid or lace). Press trim around edge of soap, forming a decorative border. Let glue dry.

Place sterno can in fondue dish base. Break or cut paraffin into small pieces. Place in tin can.(A tuna fish can works nicely.) Light sterno. When wax is melted, paint 1 coat of wax over entire front surface of soap. Work quickly using long, even strokes.

Apply a second coat if needed. (See figure 9-2.)

teaching tips

If your class is "arty," they can paint on their own designs with acrylic. When the paint dries, frost according to waxing directions in the previous section.

Frosted soap can also be displayed on an Easy Easel. (See page 36 for directions.)

Because of hot wax and burning sterno can, close supervision is necessary with this activity.

Ask students to bring 1 or 2 bars of soap from home.

If wax gets too hot during the activity, extinguish sterno can by replacing the lid. Let wax cool; then relight. This method is safer than removing can of melted wax from the fondue base.

figure 9-2   *Jack Frost's Soap Art*

It is best not to use new paint brushes since the wax is hard to remove. Save old paint brushes for another frosty day.

evaluation

Neatness; design; wax application; and overall effect of completed craft.

Nylon Net Scrubber

—frilly, fluffy ball makes scrubbing fun!

materials

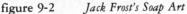

- 1½ yards nylon net
- needle (large eye)
- strong thread
- bone ring (or pull tab from soft drink can)
- scissors
- yardstick

Cut nylon net into strips 1½ yards long and 4½" wide.

Thread needle with double strand of strong thread, and knot thread in center of 1 end of net. Gather net by taking big stitches down center of net strip. When you reach the end, push net together. This forms a ball.

Push needle back through all layers of net; repeat; and secure with knot. Do not cut thread yet.

Slip needle through bone ring. Wrap thread around ring 4 or 5 times. Shove needle back through ball, and tie a knot. Fluff net. Trim uneven edges and leftover thread with scissors. (See figure 9-3.)

figure 9-3   *Nylon Net Scrubber*

teaching tips

Students may want to use more than 1 color of net. (It's a good way to use up scraps.)

Cut net into strips equaling 1½ yards in length and gather.

Kindergarten and first-graders may need help tying their knots.

Older students may want to tie their fluffy pompons on their shoe skates.

Whip up a scrubber for the classroom while the kids are busy. It's unbeatable for removing clay, glue and paint from hands, fingers, sinks and countertops.

evaluation

Fullness and shape of completed scrubber.

Fall Fantasy Candle

—ice water explodes melted wax into unique, ornate candles!

materials

- candle wax (Granulated type melts faster.)
- old boiler pan
- empty 1 lb. coffee can
- electric stove burner (or gas camp stove)
- old candles (at least 5″ tall)
- ice cubes (or frozen ice pack used in camping coolers)
- water
- large container at least 8″ deep (like metal potato chip can, wastepaper basket or water bath canner)
- old or broken crayons (with labels removed)
- aluminum pie pans (various sizes)
- lined rubber (or protective) gloves
- artificial flowers (fall colors)
- glitter (optional)
- matches
- newspapers

Cover work area with newspapers. Fill boiler pan approximately ½ full of water and place on stove burner.

Place wax in coffee can (about ½ full), and set can in middle of water-filled pan. To color wax, add a few broken crayons to can. Each color will require a different can for purity.

While wax melts, secure one 5″ candle to bottom center of aluminum pie pan. (Melt bottom of candle slightly with lighted match to melt wax; then set candle in wax puddle.) Fill large container (canner or chip can) ½ full of ice cubes. Water is added later.

When wax is melted, allow to heat a few more minutes. Add water to large container filled with ice. (You will have to judge water depth. It should not cover the top 2″ of a 5″ candle.)

Wearing rubber gloves, pour wax into pie pan around candle; fill pan ⅔ full. Pick up sides of pan and set it on surface of ice water. Set a second or 2, allowing candle to become sealed to plate. (See figure 9-4a.)

Now, grasp top of candle (upper 2″) and twisting and turning, quickly push pan into icy water. This action causes the hot wax to explode as it is immersed, and it hardens almost instantaneously. (See figure 9-4b.) Remove candle from water. (See figure 9-4c.) Turn upside down and shake out excess water; then set candle on newspaper. If desired, sprinkle on glitter.

When completely cool, remove candle from pie pan. If it won't release, hold

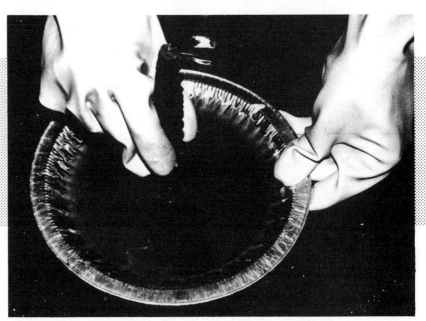

figure 9-4a   *Fall Fantasy Candle—skim pan on top of icy*
water for a second to adhere candle to pan.

figure 9-4b   *Plunge into icy water using a twisting and turning action.*

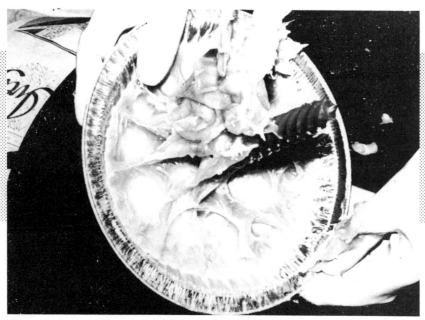

figure 9-4c   *Remove exploded candle from water.*

sideways over sink and allow hot tap water to run over bottom of pan for a few minutes.

Now decorate base of candle with colorful artificial fall flowers, leaves, acorns or tiny forest animals. (See figure 9-4d.)

figure 9-4d   *Fall Fantasy Candle—Autumn all year long in hues of orange, brown and gold.*

teaching tips

This is not a quick craft, but it is fun and rewarding. Exercise extreme caution during this activity. Dip only 1 candle at a time. Students will enjoy watching and will be happy to wait their turn. [*Note: do not heat wax over a direct flame and always wear protective rubber gloves.*]

No 2 candles will be exactly alike. If your candle does not explode, the water may not be cold enough; or the wax may not be hot enough. Or, perhaps you are not filling the pie pan full enough with wax.

Experiment! If your candle is a "dud," tear off excess wax, put it in can, remelt, fill pie pan and redip.

The size of the pie pan determines the diameter of the complete candle. Individual pot pie pans make ideal small candles, the perfect size for small children.

Even though they should not dip their own candles, young students will enjoy watching you make them, and they'll have fun decorating their cooled candles.

Seasonal changes are a snap! Color wax and decorate candles with appropriate holiday or seasonal colors. (See figure 9-4e.)

figure 9-4e   *Red wax and candle decorated with vivid green holly sprigs and glitter makes a colorful Christmas candle.*

evaluation

Students who dip candles themselves—design; explosive effect; color selection; and decoration.

Younger students—suitability of candle decorations to theme presented.

Windy March Fan

—big enough to stir up a cool breeze; small enough to slip inside a pocket or purse.

materials

- 4 empty plastic gallon milk jugs (washed and dried)
- lightweight cardboard (The side of a shoe box works nicely.)

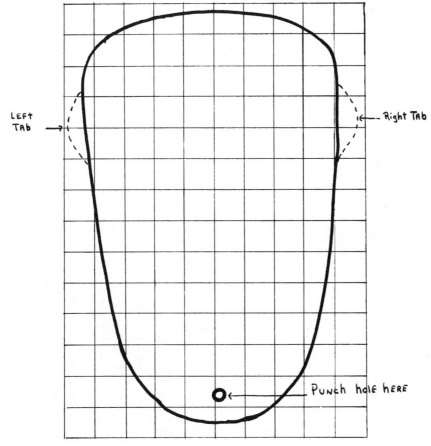

figure 9-5a   *Pattern for Windy March Fan*

- scissors
- dark crayon
- tempera paint (fingernail polish or small decals)
- brass fastener
- clear fingernail polish
- carbon paper
- paper punch

Enlarge and cut out bell-shaped fan pattern on a piece of lightweight cardboard. (See figure 9-5a.) See page 28 for pattern-enlarging techniques.

Place pattern on 1 side of milk jug. Use crayon to trace pattern piece. Draw all 4 bells needed for fan; then, cut out 2 bells. On third bell, draw a half circle on the outside, right-hand side about 2 inches down from widest part (top) of bell. Circle should be about the size of your thumb. Draw an identical half circle on fourth bell, but place it on left-hand side. (2 half circles make thumb tab pull-outs to open fan.)

Use paper punch to make a hole in center of each bell ¾" up from the bottom. Punched holes should be centered on each cut bell.

Assemble fan. Place bell with half circle on left on flat surface. Add 2 plain bells, and place final bell with half circle on right on top. Push brass fastener through all 4 holes and fasten.

Decorate fan with paint or fingernail polish. If tempera is used, let paint dry; then coat with clear fingernail polish to protect design. (See figure 9-5b.)

Young, less artistic students can decorate their fans with decals.

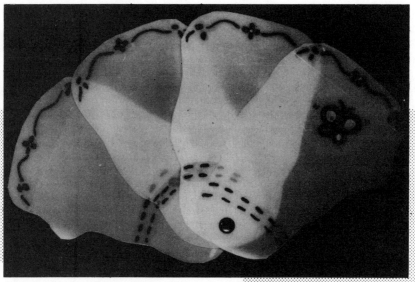

figure 9-5b   *Windy March Fan*

teaching tips

Young students might have difficulty cutting out patterns. Sharp scissors are essential, so it may be safer to pre-cut pattern for them. They can assemble and decorate.

Other large plastic containers, such as detergent bottles and floor polish jugs, can be used too. Try to avoid containers with indented designs or excessive printing. (See page 190 to remove advertising print.)

evaluation

Originality of design; neatness; exactness of holes through which brass fastener is inserted; and overall appearance.

Summer/Winter Tile Trivet

—tricky trivet makes a practical welcome gift.

materials

- 1 4¼″ × 4¼″ ceramic tile square
- small bowl of water
- small decals (available in variety or hardware stores)
- 4 marbles
- sponge (or paper towel)
- white glue
- newspaper

Cover work area with newspaper. Turn ceramic tile upside down, and glue 1 marble in each corner. Allow glue to dry.

Turn tile right side up. (Marbles become legs.) Follow decal application directions. Slip decal on trivet, and wipe off excess water. (See figure 9-6.)

teaching tips

This is a very simple craft, which can be made and taken home the same day. Young children really enjoy it because it is easy and produces a fine, attractive and useful gift.

Older students will also enjoy making this easy activity. Clever, unique or ecological decals are essential to capture their imagination and to add to the appeal of this activity.

The trivet is super for hot and cold dishes and makes an excellent potted plant stand. Or, you can adhere a cloth wall hanger to the back of the tile for a captivating wall plaque.

figure 9-6   *Summer/Winter Tile Trivet*

evaluation

Placement of marbles; decal application; and general appearance.

Elegant Egg Pin Cushion

—no one will know this sewing helper was hatched from a plastic egg!

materials

- any color large plastic egg (kind pantyhose come in)
- 2 bone rings (used to hang cafe curtains)
- epoxy glue (The 5-minute kind is best.)
- ½ plastic foam ball (should fit inside egg half)
- 4″ × 4″ piece of felt (color coordinated with color of egg)
- assortment of ribbon scraps
- artificial flowers, rick-rack, nylon net scraps
- rubber band
- plastic knife (used for mixing glue)

Open egg, and set both halves flat side down on table. Mix small amount of epoxy glue. (Jar lid works well.)

Smear glue on 1 side of bone ring. Set on top of round end of egg half. Repeat with second egg half. Hold rings in place until glue sets. (They will slide off if they can.)

Lay felt on table. Set rounded half of foam ball on top of felt, and fold felt around ball. Tuck covered ball inside 1 plastic egg half. (Either half works.)

Spread glue on top of 1 bone ring. (You will have to mix another small batch.) Set glued ring on top of other bone ring, making sure felt-covered ball is on top. Hold until glue sets.

Decorate pin cushion by gluing rick-rack, fancy braid or glitter around top edge. Tie a pretty ribbon around the middle (where egg halves join) to cover bone rings. (See figure 9-7.)

figure 9-7   *Elegant Egg Pin Cushion—rick-rack and ribbon trim or fancy nylon net skirt*

teaching tips

Young children may need assistance when they cover foam ball with felt and when they insert it into egg half.

A fluffy nylon net skirt can easily be added. Cut strip of net 3½" wide and 12" long. Gather net around bone rings in middle, and secure with rubber band. Stick artificial flowers into rubber band.

Blue or gold eggs can become a handy tie tac holder for Dad. Wrap a felt neck tie around joined bone rings, and add a glittered or jeweled tie tac.

evaluation

Originality; decoration; color coordination; and overall attractiveness of completed craft.

Cracked Marble Creatures

—wide, wiggly eyes enhance these crystal clear creatures!

materials

- crystal clear marbles (or other transparent colors)
- quick-drying cement (or 5-minute epoxy)
- scraps of felt
- wax paper (or newspaper)
- small, wiggly eyes (found in craft supply stores)
- cookie sheet
- ice cubes
- electric stove burner (or oven)
- boiler pan
- towel
- water (in sink or old pan)

Cover bottom of boiler pan with marbles. Turn burner temperature to high. Place towel in bottom of sink (or old pan), and fill sink (or pan) ½ full of water. Add 2 or more trays of ice cubes.

Place marbles atop stove burner. Allow to get hot (approximately 10 minutes); then remove from burner. Drop marbles immediately into ice water. The towel prevents them from breaking open. The marbles should crack as soon as they hit the water. If not, they weren't hot enough, and process must be repeated.

When marbles cool, remove from water and dry. (You can also heat them in an oven at 500 degrees for 1 or 2 minutes, then drop in ice water to crack.)

Cover work area with wax paper (or newspaper). Keep marbles in tin can (or box) so they don't roll on the floor.

Glue marbles together to create cracked creatures. Quick-drying cement requires a little holding time; 5-minute epoxy works best. Epoxy allows older students to work quickly, but dries almost too fast for younger students.

Some creatures to make: Charlie Caterpillar, Barney Beagle, and Sammy Squirt.

Charlie Caterpillar takes 6 marbles. (See figure 9-8a.) First, glue 1 marble to the top of another. Let glue set. Add 1 marble at a time to bottom marble until Charlie is 5 marbles long. Glue a wiggly eye on each side of his head and a felt necktie under his chin, and glue on paper-punched felt polka dots and a genuine acorn cap.

Barney Beagle takes 7 marbles. (See figure 9-8b.) Set 1 marble on wax paper, and glue 5 marbles around center marble. This forms Barney's 4 legs and head.

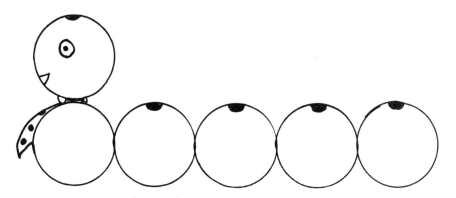

figure 9-8a   *Cracked Marble Creatures—Charlie Caterpillar*

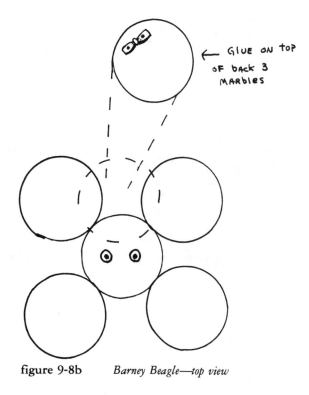

← GIUE ON toP
oF bAck 3
MARbIes

figure 9-8b   *Barney Beagle—top view*

When glue is set, glue final marble on top of 2 hind-leg marbles for elevated tail. Wiggly eyes and brown felt, floppy ears make Barney lovable. If he's tired give him a dangling, red felt tongue; or if he's just home from the groomers, give him a bright green felt ribbon for the tip of his tail.

Sammy Squirt is a basic creature figure and a good character with which to begin this activity. (See figure 9-8c.) Glue 4 marbles together (forming a square shape). When glue sets, top with 1 marble in center. Sammy is a tiny fellow who

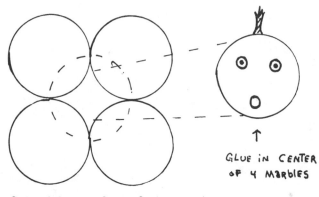

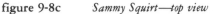

GLUE IN CENTER
OF 4 MARBLES

figure 9-8c   *Sammy Squirt—top view*

figure 9-8d   *Cracked Marble Creatures—left to right: Barney Beagle, Sammy Squirt on top of the world and Charlie, the polka-dotted caterpillar sunbathing on piece of driftwood*

can perch almost anywhere. Don't forget his all-seeing wiggly eyes and his yarn curl hair. Change Sammy into Samantha by topping with an upside-down artificial flower. (See figure 9-8d.)

teaching tips

Uncracked marbles will work; however, they do not produce the same interesting effect as their cracked peers.

A nature hike can provide an abundance of creature props. Attach critters to rocks with a pinch of clay; or rest them on a piece of driftwood or walnut shell mountains.

There is no limit to the combination of marbles to create cracked creatures. Let students make up their own designs. (See figure 9-8e.)

figure 9-8e   *Patterns for other Cracked Marble Creatures*

If the class is studying foreign lands and customs, they can dress their creatures in proper attire. Make stand-up cardboard backgrounds or flags, and put creatures on display. Children can view each character and guess what country it represents.

evaluation

Originality; humor; neatness; attire; and method of display.

chapter ten —

Crafts for Various Special Seasons

Everyone loves special holidays and seasons! The activities in this chapter will delight your students and give you an excellent opportunity to elaborate on the background and history of each special occasion.

Educational values in this chapter are endless. Students can learn as much about various national and international holidays and the 4 seasons as you desire. The activities will also develop their manual dexterity, sense of design, self-expression and depth of perception.

May Day Basket

—fill with spring flowers or tasty treats to celebrate the coming of spring!

materials

- plastic detergent bottle (Remove label, wash and dry.)
- scissors
- Easter grass
- ribbon scraps (½" width or less)
- paper punch
- felt-tipped pens (kind that write on anything)
- ruler
- dark crayon

Measure 3" up from bottom of bottle, and sketch a 3" line around base of bottle. Turn bottle so 1 side seam faces you; then measure ½" width (center on side

figure 10-1a   *May Day Basket*

seam). Now, measure 6″ up side of bottle. (See figure 10-1b.) Repeat on opposite side. (Side strips become basket handle.)

Use sketch line and make half triangles on front and back of bottle. This makes a fancy border. Cut along crayon line with sharp scissors. Cut out half triangles and handle strips.

Punch a hole in each end of handle strips, placing 1 strip on top of other matching holes. Insert ribbon scrap through holes, and tie in pretty bow.

Decorate outside with felt-tipped pens or fingernail polish. Then fill basket with colorful artificial or paper flowers. (See figure 10-1a.)

teaching tips

Young students will need a helping hand drawing and cutting the basket.

To switch seasons, add Easter grass and candy eggs; fill a white basket with Valentine candy and decorate with red felt hearts; or make a Jack O' Lantern face and fill with Halloween treats.

Bottles make quick vases. Simply cut off top about 2″ down from cap. Decorate by gluing cut-out magazine (or greeting card) pictures on front. Perk up the classroom, library or cafeteria with cheerful basket and vases filled with flowers.

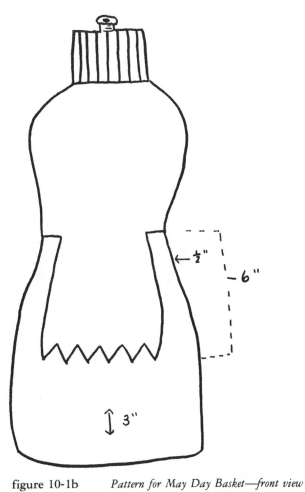

figure 10-1b   *Pattern for May Day Basket—front view*

evaluation

Cutting; neatness; decoration; and overall, finished product.

Spring Berry Basket Bird Cage

—this cheerful bird in a gilded cage can adorn classroom, patio or tree limb.

materials

- scissors
- fine wire (Picture hanging wire will do.)

- 2 alike plastic berry baskets (kind small tomatoes and strawberries come in)
- artificial flowers
- ribbon scraps (or yarn or gold cord)
- feathery bird (or butterfly or bumblebee)

Turn 1 basket upside down on flat surface, and tie a bow in middle of basket (outside bottom).

Then turn basket right side up. Use wire to attach artificial flowers and bird (or butterfly or bumblebee) to inside bottom center of basket. (This is bottom of bird cage.)

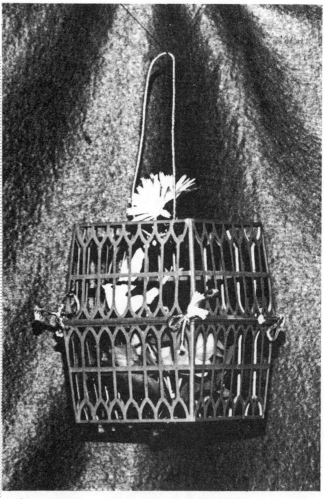

figure 10-2   *Spring Berry Basket Bird Cage*

Turn second basket upside-down. (This will be top of cage.) In the center, tie a long yarn loop (or pretty ribbon or gold cord). This is the hanger. Decorate around loop by wiring more flowers in place.

Set top basket (with loop) on top of bottom basket (containing bird). Join basket corners with yarn (ribbon or cord) bows. Cut yarn about 5" long. Thread through top and bottom basket corners, and tie in a bow. Repeat in other 3 corners.

Hang cage in 1 corner of room, dangle outside on low tree limb or place in front of classroom window. (See figure 10-2.)

teaching tips

Small children may need a helping hand to secure flowers and tie yarn loop and bows.

If you're studying birds, have each student draw a different species on heavy white paper. Cut out and color; then glue on real feathers. Place bird in his cage, and let children describe their feathered friend, what he likes to eat, the color of female and where the bird lives. Cages can be hung on a classroom clothesline for everyone to see.

evaluation

Placement of flowers; color coordination; neatness; ribbon tying; and originality.

Egg Carton Christmas Tree

—a sparkling way to decorate mantle, desk or holiday party table!

materials

- 1 12"-tall plastic foam tree form
- 1 pedestal type base (glass or metal)
- 1 bottle glitter (any color)
- white glue
- 2 packs fancy sequins (any color)
- 1 box pearl-headed straight pins
- 6 alike plastic egg cartons (all the same color)
- scissors
- newspaper
- florist clay

- 1 egg carton (or muffin tin) to hold glue

Cover work area with newspaper. Cut lids from 6 egg cartons. (Save lids—students can use them to catch glitter and to make tree topping stars.)

Then cut out each section of egg carton, and trim edges of each cup.

To make petals, cut "V" shape in each side of the cup. Cut out all petals. (See figure 10-3a.) Spread a small amount of glue on each petal tip, and sprinkle on glitter. Allow to dry. Then glitter all petals.

figure 10-3a   *Egg Carton Petals—cut, glitter tips, insert*
pin through sequin and center of cup.

Attach tree form to pedestal base with florist clay; and 1 at a time, push pearl-headed pin through 1 fancy sequin. Push pin through center of 1 egg cup. Stick egg cup into top of tree form.

Stick pin through another sequin and push through egg cup. Stick into tree form side—*working from the top down*. Place cups close together, while at the same time, being careful not to crush any egg cups already on tree form. Continue until tree form is completely covered with glittered egg cups.

Top tree with a star. To make, draw a pattern on newspaper. Then transfer pattern to top of egg carton lid, and cut out star. Smear star with glue and sprinkle on glitter. When dry, glitter other side of star. Allow to dry.

Remove head from 1 pin. Stick into star (between points). Remove pearl-headed pin from top egg cup. Insert pin with attached star. (See figure 10-3b.)

teaching tips

This is a fun, easy craft that students will enjoy. Small children will catch on

figure 10-3b *Egg Carton Christmas Tree*

easily after seeing a sample and being shown how to cut petals and insert pin and sequin. They may need some help making the star.

Glittered cups can be used to decorate other form shapes, such as wreaths and large round balls. To hang balls, attach a piece of fishing line to form base with a pin dipped in glue.

Tiny Christmas balls, plastic holly and colorful ribbons can be inserted inside or between egg cups to decorate or fill in blank spaces.

evaluation

General workmanship; neatness; cutting; glittering; and overall uniformity of tree.

Friendly Halloween Ghost

—playful little trick-or-treater!

materials

- 2 sheets white facial tissue
- scissors
- strong white thread
- black, felt-tipped marking pen

Spread out 1 sheet of facial tissue on flat surface. Roll second sheet of tissue between hands, and shape into a ball.

Set ball in middle of tissue on flat surface. Gather first sheet of tissue around ball. (This is ghost's head.) Tie with strong white thread around "neck." Draw eyes and mouth on ghost head with marking pen. (See figure 10-4.)

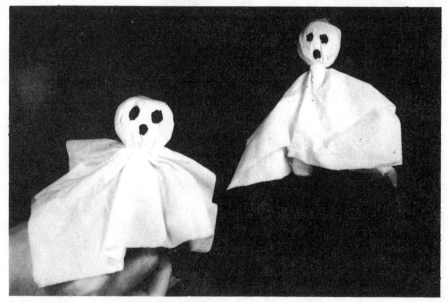

figure 10-4   *Friendly Halloween Ghost*

teaching tips

Friendly ghost can dance around the room by hanging from ceiling with invisible thread, or turn him into a puppet. Tape invisible thread to back of head for dancing puppet, or make a finger puppet by leaving room around neck when tying with thread.

Young students will need help tying their thread.

evaluation

Roundness of head; and facial features.

Valentine Topiary Tree

—paper hearts and tiny flowers make this tree a perfect valentine!

materials

- 1 small paper drinking cup
- ½ cup fruit dough (See page 185 for recipe.)
- ½"-wide red satin ribbon (approximately ½ yard)
- gold glitter
- white glue
- florist wire
- new pencil (sharpened)
- red construction paper
- red toothpicks
- cellophane tape
- scissors
- tiny artificial flowers and leaves
- old newspapers

Draw 6 to 10 hearts (about ½" long) on red construction paper, and cut them out. Tape a toothpick on each heart.

Cut ends of artificial flower and leaf stems at an angle. (This makes for easy insertion into foam ball.) Then push sharpened end of pencil into foam ball. Shove pencil point in at least 1½" or until ball is secure. Stick leaves and flowers into ball 1 at a time. When ball is full, stick in Valentine heart toothpicks. Set aside.

Cover work area with newspaper. Make a line of white glue around top of paper cup, and sprinkle on gold glitter. Set aside to dry.

Make (or prepare in advance) fruit dough. (See page 186 for directions.) Fill paper cup ⅔ full with dough. Stick eraser end of pencil into dough. Be sure pencil is centered in cup and pushed down far enough so topiary tree is not top heavy.

Next, make 2 ribbon bows. Loop 9″ of red satin ribbon, gather in center and tie with florist wire. Make second bow identical.

Push wire of 1 bow into flour dough at pencil base. Then turn cup around, and push second bow into dough. (See figure 10-5.)

figure 10-5   *Valentine Topiary Tree*

teaching tips

Young students will need a little help cutting their flower and leaf stems and inserting pencil point into foam ball properly.

Make giant trees by anchoring foam balls on a pole in sand-filled flower pots. Balance trees by adorning with larger flowers and leaves, or insert live greenery and adorn with large paper hearts or flowers. Trees can be used to decorate school office, cafeteria or stage.

Students can make 1-sided trees for Valentine cards, bulletin boards and classroom doors. For small trees, cut foam ball in half and substitute a soda straw for the pencil and cut paper cup in half. Glue to paper plates, meat trays, wooden planks or felt for wall hanging.

Glue 1 ribbon bow to base of half tree; then glue half cup in place.

evaluation

Uniformity of design; neatness; balance; and overall effect of completed tree.

Thanksgiving Horn Full of Plenty

—a bountiful harvest of holiday fruits!

materials

- old newspaper
- brown enamel spray paint
- scissors
- cellophane tape
- pipe cleaners
- tempera paint (assorted colors)
- paint brush
- 1 spray can of clear varnish
- wax paper
- tiny twigs
- artificial leaves (from old plastic flowers)
- florist tape
- 1 batch fruit dough

First, prepare fruit dough according to the following recipe. (One batch made all samples in photograph, figure 10-6.)

fruit dough recipe

- measuring cup
- measuring spoons
- 1 large bowl (or plastic dishpan)
- 1 long-handled wooden spoon
- 3 cups regular flour
- 1½ cups salt

- 1½ tsp. powdered alum (found in drugstores)
- ¾ to 1 cup water
- old newspaper
- wax paper
- cookie sheet (optional)

figure 10-6   *Thanksgiving Horn Full of Plenty—complete
with fruit dough recipe*

Cover work area with newspaper. Combine all dry ingredients in bowl, adding a small amount of water at a time; mix well with spoon or hands. Work mixture until it has the consistency of biscuit dough. Take care not to use too much water since fruit will not hold its shape and will take longer to dry.

Shape portions of dough into fruit forms. Set finished fruit on wax paper to dry, and push twig stems into fruit while dough is soft. (Dried dough is very hard.) Stick pipe cleaner stems into grapes and cherries to cluster later. (To insert in a foam base, stick 1 toothpick into each fruit while it is soft.)

Let fruit dry. It will take a day or 2 in warm weather. Humid or rainy weather will prolong drying. If you are in a hurry, place fruit on a cookie sheet and dry in oven set at 200 degrees. Dry until fruit is powder white and hard. Allow oven-dried fruit to cool before painting.

Paint dried fruit with tempera. When paint dries, spray fruit with clear varnish.

Join grapes with florist tape to form bunch. Use tape to attach leaves. Then arrange dough fruit in horn of plenty for Thanksgiving centerpiece.

To make Horn of Plenty, lay 2 thicknesses of double-paged newspaper on a flat surface. Begin rolling lower right-hand corner into cone shape. Roll paper, keeping the lower end tight while broadening the upper end of the cone opening.

Roll all the paper; then secure lower right end with cellophane tape. Put hand inside cone and expand upper, open end if necessary. Secure newspaper edges with tape.

Insert a pipe cleaner into pointed tip of horn. Bend pipe cleaner to curl horn end. Wad up 1 single sheet of newspaper, and push into cone. This helps horn hold its shape. Trim newspaper edges around horn opening; then fold back 1" of paper to form lip around opening.

Place finished horn on newspaper, and spray with brown enamel paint. Follow paint label directions. Horn may require 2 or 3 coats of paint for good coverage. Allow paint to dry. Fill horn with painted dough fruit.

teaching tips

Young students may need help rolling and shaping their horns.

When preparing dough, follow warning on alum label. Children should not eat dough or put unwashed hands in their mouth.

Real fruit or pictures will help students paint realistic fruit.

Fruit dough has many classroom uses since it hardens without cooking or baking. Dough can be colored with food coloring or acrylic during mixing. Students can make way-out creatures, bumblebees, shape mountains and volcanos; they can even mold prehistoric dinosaurs or roll dough thin and cut with cookie cutters for Christmas tree ornaments and jeweled pins. Wrap leftover dough in wax paper, and store in refrigerator; it will keep several days.

evaluation

Shape of horn; arrangement of fruit; painting; shape of individual fruit; and overall, completed Horn Full of Plenty.

Abraham Lincoln's Book Buddy

—the long tail marks the spot where you stop!

materials

- assorted colors of felt
- paper punch
- white glue
- scissors
- ball point pen

• lightweight cardboard (A dress box works nicely.)

Make and cut out cardboard mouse pattern. (See figure 10-7a.) To enlarge, see page 28. Place pattern on felt, trace and cut out. Punch out eyes and nose of felt, and cut out ears and whiskers. Glue facial features in place and let glue dry. (See figure 10-7b.)

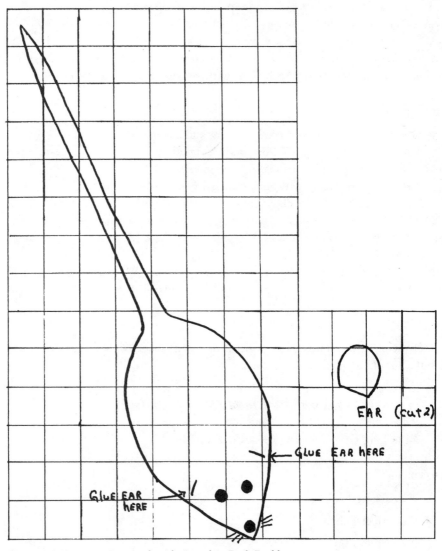

figure 10-7a   *Pattern for Abe Lincoln's Book Buddy*

figure 10-7b   *Abe Lincoln's Book Buddy*

teaching tips

It is easier and quicker if basic mouse pattern is cut in advance for younger students.

evaluation

Accuracy of pattern design; cutting; placement of facial features; and originality.

Easter Bunny Basket

—fluffy cotton balls glamourize this sturdy Easter basket.

materials

- 1 round, plastic jug (A milk jug or bleach bottle works nicely.)
- sharp scissors
- dark crayon
- felt-tipped marking pens (kind that writes on anything)

- cotton balls
- felt scraps
- white glue
- Easter egg grass
- ruler (or cloth tape measure)
- 2 brass fasteners
- teaspoon (optional)
- paper punch
- automatic dishwashing detergent (optional)
- paper towels

Wash and dry jug. Measure 4″ (or any height you like) up from bottom of jug, and draw a cutting line with crayon. Measure 1½″ above the 4″ line. (This will become basket handle.) Draw a cutting line.

Cut along crayon lines. Cut 1 side of handle so you have a long, continuous strip. Decorate handle with felt-tipped pens, rick-rack or decorative braid.

If handle has printed advertisement, remove by mixing a small amount of automatic dishwashing detergent with water to form a thick paste. Spread paste over letters and set aside. In an hour or so, detergent will soften letters. Scrap off with edge of a teaspoon; then wash and dry handle and decorate.

Punch a hole in each end of handle about ½″ in from the end. Punch a hole in each side of jug (directly opposite each other). Then insert a brass fastener through the hole in jug, then handle, and spread fastener wings. Handle ends should be inside basket. Attach other side of handle.

Decorate outside of basket with cotton balls. Spread white glue on small section of basket at a time. Press cotton balls into glue 1 at a time, covering entire basket. While glue dries, cut out felt rabbit eyes, mouth, nose and whiskers. Glue in place.

Fill basket with Easter grass. (See figure 10-8.)

teaching tips

Any size or type of plastic container will make dandy, safe baskets. Large baskets make delightful spring centerpieces.

Baskets should be pre-cut for students in kindergarten through third grade.

These durable baskets will also make terrific Halloween trick-or-treat containers. Spray with orange enamel paint. When dry, glue black felt jack-o-lantern features in place.

Baskets also make handy classroom crayon, chalk and pencil containers. Students can decorate with their names, magazine pictures or alphabet letters.

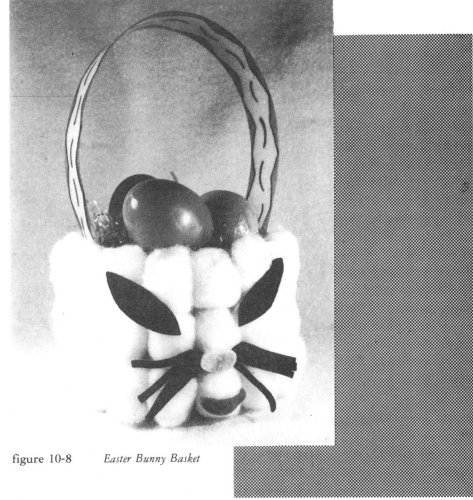

figure 10-8   *Easter Bunny Basket*

evaluation

Cutting; gluing; uniformity of cotton balls; facial design; handle decoration; neatness; and proportion.

chapter eleven —

New Ways to Trim a Christmas Tree

This chapter is designed to help you cope with the holiday season by providing an abundance of holiday craft activities for your students. Many scrap items can be turned into glittering ornaments. Start collecting basic supplies as soon as school starts, and store in cardboard boxes.

When working with glue or paint, always cover work areas with old newspaper for easy clean-up. And, set each container of glitter inside a different paper plate for students to work over. Use pipe cleaners, paper clips, thread, florist wire, fishing line, garbage or bread bag twist ties to hang ornaments. Review the activities in preceding chapters, and see which ones can be transformed into clever tree trimmers.

Have students initial all their ornaments so when school recesses for the holidays they can claim their ornaments, take them home, and hang them on their family trees. Or, students can elect to give their decorated classroom tree to a nursing home, church, children's home or hospital youth ward.

Educational values in this chapter include manual dexterity, perspective, spatial relations, design, color coordination, imagination, cutting, shapes, proportion, physical coordination and sharing.

Crepe Paper Christmas Tree

—frilly green pompons adorn this festive holiday tree!

materials

- 3 packages of green crepe paper
- scissors

- cellophane tape
- ruler
- florist wire
- approximately 40 wire coat hangers
- wire cutters
- artificial tree centerpost and base (Centerpost in photograph is 28″ long excluding base.)
- broomstick (optional)
- electric drill (optional)
- gallon-sized tin can (optional)
- plaster of Paris or sand (optional)

The easiest way to create this lovely, inexpensive Christmas tree is to utilize a used, artificial Christmas tree centerpost and base. The holes are already drilled at the proper angle, and the base is intact.

All coat hanger wire branches for this tree are cut 15″ in length. However, if you cannot obtain a used, artificial tree centerpost you can make your own. (Note optional items under **materials**.)

Cut a broomstick into a piece 36″ long. The 8″ required to insert stick into a can base is included in the 36″. Drill approximately 40 holes in broomstick at varying intervals. Drill holes at an angle to prevent wire branches from falling out. Select a drill bit slightly larger in circumference than wire; then drill 1 hole in center of cut end of stick for top branch.

Stick uncut end (top of broomstick) into a painted or paper-covered tin can. Anchor stick by filling can with sand or plaster of Paris.

Cut approximately 40 coat hanger wire branches 15″ long. (Cut off bottom of coat hanger to make branches.) Stick branches into holes in tree centerpost. Now, shape tree by cutting upper and middle branches a shorter length. (Branches cut for artificial tree centerpost do not require shaping.)

After the tree centerpost is assembled, decorate each wire branch. Cut a single layer of crepe paper 14″ long and 1½″ wide. Cut a ¾″ fringe border along 1 side of crepe paper. Then remove a branch from tree, holding coat hanger branch in your right hand. Place unfringed edge of crepe paper strip against top of wire. Secure with a small piece of tape. (See figure 11-1a.)

Wrap paper strip around and around wire until you reach the bottom. Then secure paper end to wire with tape. (Unfringed side of paper must be against wire when wrapping, or fringe will not fluff out on branch.) Cover all branches. [*Note: if all the branches are the same length you can remove them all from centerpost. However, if they are different lengths, take care when removing and be sure to reinsert branch in the proper hole. You can paint tip ends different colors to denote length.*]

Stick covered branches in centerpost and make pompon foliage. You will

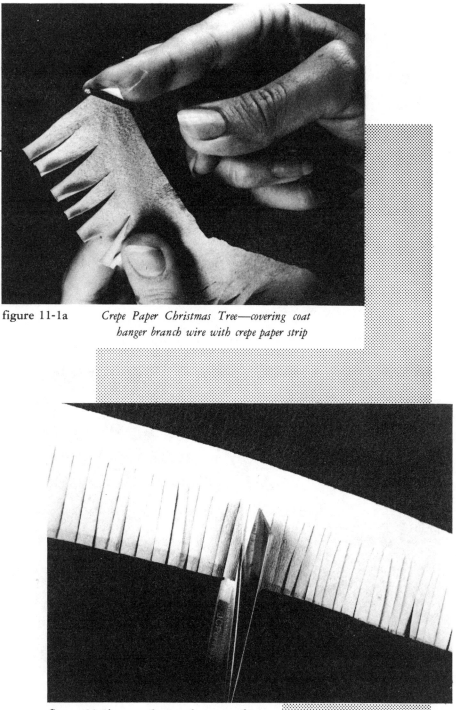

figure 11-1a   *Crepe Paper Christmas Tree—covering coat
hanger branch wire with crepe paper strip*

figure 11-1b   *Cutting the pompon fringe*

figure 11-1c   *Securing wire to center of gathered pompon*

figure 11-1d   *Pinching sides of pompon together at bottom to
complete one pompon*

need 1 pompon for each branch of tree. To make a pompon, cut a single layer of crepe paper 4" wide and 12" long. Fold paper in half along 12" length. Cut a 1-½" fringe border along unfolded edge of paper through both layers. (See figure 11-1b.)

Unfold cut paper. Use fingers to gather paper, and tie center of gathered paper with a 6" piece of florist wire. (See figure 11-1c.)

Pinch both sides of pompon together at the bottom, pushing sides together to form 1 large pompon. (See figure 11-1d.) Twist wire of pompon around tip end of branch; continue until each branch has a pompon attached to it.

Make approximately 18 more pompons. Tie gathered middles with 12" pieces of wire. Tie pompons around tree centerpost to add fullness to tree and to hide stick.

Tree is now ready to decorate. (See figure 11-1e.)

figure 11-1e   *Decorated Crepe Paper Christmas Tree*

teaching tips

After the holidays, dismantle the tree and remove all the crepe paper. Store centerpost and branches in a box until next year. Each new class of students will enjoy covering the branches and making the pompon foliage.

Students can bring coat hangers from home, or perhaps a laundry will donate them.

If wrapping fringe around wire branches is too difficult for young students, spray paint centerpost and branches green. Students can make pompons and tie in place.

Decorated 28″ tree centerpost, excluding base, will stand approximately 40″ tall.

evaluation

Covering of branches; pompons; fullness and visual effect of completed tree.

Soda Straw and Bead Garland

—colorful tree trimmers that even young students can make easily!

materials

- plastic drinking straws (Paper straws will work, too.)
- heavy white thread
- large-eyed needle
- assortment of plastic beads
- scissors

Cut straws into 2″ pieces. Use a double strand of heavy thread to string garland, and knot ends securely.

Push needle through center of a straw piece. Slip on a bead, another straw, etc. until the garland reaches the desired length. Drape garland on Christmas tree. (See figure 11-2.)

teaching tips

Plastic straws are easier to work with and will retain their shape longer than paper straws. Use colored straws for a prettier garland.

Each student can make a section of the garland, which can be tied together into 1 long strand.

Even kindergarten students will be able to make this easy tree decoration.

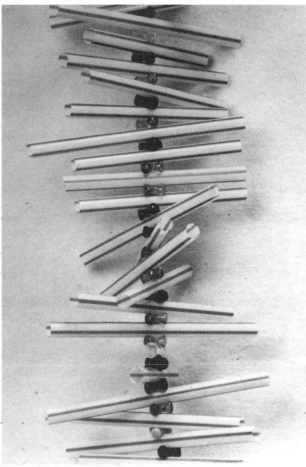

figure 11-2   *Soda Straw and Bead Garland*

evaluation

Assembly of garland; and use of colors.

Santa's Helper

—students can lend Santa a hand with these elf-like ornaments!

materials

- 1 ladies stocking (or ½ pantyhose)
- 2 satin-covered foam Christmas balls (the same color)

- strong thread
- ribbon scraps
- 2 wiggly eyes
- plastic foam meat tray
- pencil
- scissors
- felt scraps
- 1 cotton ball
- straight pins
- glitter
- white glue
- scrap of white paper
- Christmas ornament hanger

Remove ornament hanging hooks, if any, from both satin balls. Tie toe end of stocking with thread; tie securely. Then put both satin balls into toe of stocking. (Be sure 1 ball is exactly on top of the other.) Now, tie off top of stocking with thread as close to top satin ball as possible.

Cut off excess stocking above and below satin balls. Cut a circle from red felt 3″ in circumference; decorate outside edges with glitter. Use straight pins to stick felt hat on top satin ball, and glue a cotton ball pompon on top of hat.

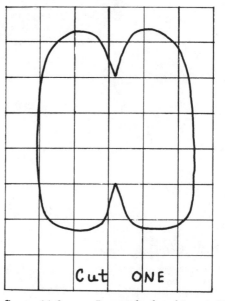

figure 11-3a   *Pattern for feet of Santa's Helper*

Glue 2 wiggly eyes on front of top satin ball; then cut a small mouth out of scrap white paper. Glue in place. Use ribbon to make a belt around center of bottom ball. Pin belt in place, and glue a red heart (or belt buckle) on front of belt.

Enlarge pattern and cut helper's feet from a foam meat tray. (See figure 11-3a.) Refer to page 28 for enlarging techniques. Use straight pins to attach feet to bottom ball.

Cut a piece of ribbon 10″ long, and fold in half lengthwise. Use a straight pin to attach ribbon ends to top satin ball; hide pin behind cotton ball. Slip an ornament hanger through ribbon loop to hang ornament on tree. (See figure 11-3b.)

figure 11-3b   *Santa's Helper*

teaching tips

White stockings with bright, red balls make ideal helpers.

Young students will need a hand tying off their stocking ends. Close supervision is recommended due to the use of straight pins.

evaluation

Facial features; decoration; and neatness.

Pill Bottle Ornament

—empty pill bottles become delicate, see-through nick-nacks to hang proudly on the tree!

materials

- any size plastic pill bottle with lid (washed and dried)
- felt scraps
- rick-rack or glitter
- decorative cord or yarn
- white glue
- scissors
- ball point pen
- small figurine (It must fit inside pill bottle.)
- small foam Christmas ball (optional)
- sequins and beads (optional)
- straight pins (optional)
- Christmas ornament hanger
- ice pick

With lid intact, set pill bottle on a piece of felt and trace around bottom and top. Cut out felt circles. Glue 1 circle on bottom of bottle. Remove lid from bottle, and glue second circle on bottle lid.

As glue dries, insert figurine in bottle. If it will not stand up properly, dab a small amount of glue on bottom of figurine before placing it in bottle.

Punch a hole through lid and felt with an ice pick. Push both ends of a strand of cord (approximately 5″ long) down through hole, and tie ends in a knot under wrong side of lid. Trim edges of lid with rick-rack, glitter or decorative braid. Let glue dry.

Place decorated lid on pill bottle. Slide a hanger onto cord loop, and hang ornament on tree. (See figure 11-4.)

teaching tips

When purchasing small figurines, take a pill bottle with you to make sure the item will fit inside.

figure 11-4   *Pill Bottle Ornament*

Tiny angels are very pretty. Glue a cotton ball inside bottle first; then glue angel on top of cotton for a "heavenly" effect.

Holes will have to be punched and the decorative cord inserted for kindergarten through third-grade students. Prepare the lids in advance, if possible. Students can glitter top of lid instead of covering it with a felt circle.

For a more fancy pill bottle ornament, older students can cut a small foam Christmas ball in half. Glue half on bottom of bottle, and glue other half on lid. Eliminate the hole in lid. Let glue dry.

Insert figurine in bottle, and place lid on bottle. Decorate foam ball sections with glitter or sequins and beads.

Stick cord loop hanger into half ball on top of bottle lid with straight pin.

evaluation

Selection of figurine; neatness; and decoration.

Candy Catcher

—children can hardly wait to complete this "tasteful" tree ornament!

materials

- large, used Christmas card
- yarn
- paper punch

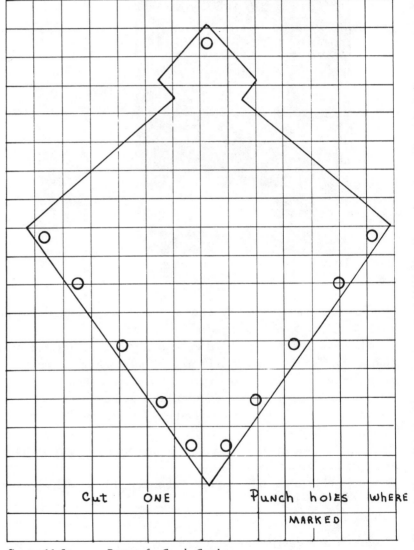

figure 11-5a   *Pattern for Candy Catcher*

- glitter
- white glue
- felt-tipped pens (or crayons)
- tracing paper (optional)
- scissors
- pencil
- Christmas ornament hanger

Make a pattern of Candy Catcher. (See figure 11-5a.) To enlarge, see page 28. Open and lay a Christmas card on a flat surface. Place pattern on front of card; then trace and cut out. Punch holes where indicated on pattern.

Color inside top of catcher if needed. (This part is back of card and is usually plain white.) Trim catcher with glitter where desired.

Insert a short strand of yarn through hanging hole, and match holes down each side of card. Lace hole together with yarn, much like lacing a shoe. Begin lacing at top of catcher and work down. Pull yarn tight to give Candy Catcher its cone shape. Tie yarn ends together at bottom.

Cut 3 strands of yarn 4″ long, and attach them to yarn ends of catcher. Tie strands in center to form a pompon fringe. Then trim uneven edges.

Attach a hanger through yarn loop at top of catcher. Fill hung catcher with candy or popcorn. (See figure 11-5b.)

figure 11-5b   *Candy Catcher*

teaching tips

Young students may need a helping hand placing pattern on card and lacing holes.

evaluation

Cutting; selection of card; decoration; and lacing.

Glittering Butterfly

—sparkling holiday baubles from clothespins and paper!

materials

- poster board
- scissors
- tracing paper (optional)
- pencil
- white glue
- assortment of glitter
- scrap of construction paper
- decorative cord
- 1 clip-type clothespin

Trace butterfly pattern onto poster board. (See figure 11-6a.) To enlarge pattern, see page 28. Cut out butterfly. Run a bead of glue around edge of butterfly wings. Be sure and leave room between wings for body of butterfly. Lay decorative cord in glue, outlining both butterfly wings with cord. Let glue dry.

Spread glue on butterfly body. (A small paint brush or cotton swab will spread glue nicely.) Sprinkle glitter in glue.

Now, glue and glitter 4 circles on butterfly wings. Let glue dry. Coat remainder of each wing with glue and glitter. Let glue dry.

Cut 2 narrow antennae from construction paper. Lay clothespin on its side, closed ends away from you. Coat the side of clothespin facing you with glue. Lay the 2 antennae in glue near closed end of pin. Center butterfly on clothespin. Let glue dry.

Clip glittering butterfly to holiday tree for sparkling ornament. (See figure 11-6b.)

teaching tips

Be sure the decorative cord is dry before applying glitter.

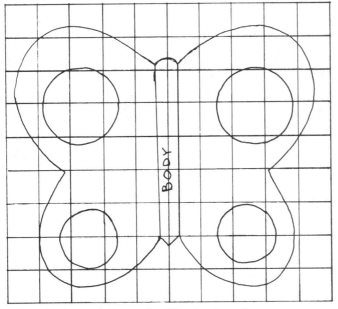

figure 11-6a   *Pattern for Glittering Butterfly*

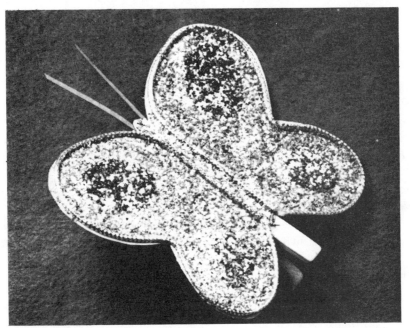

figure 11-6b   *Glittering Butterfly*

Gold or silver cord found in a craft supply store works beautifully. It is pliable and adheres quickly to the glue. Yarn could be substituted for the cord if necessary.

Various colors of glitter makes a more dramatic butterfly. Photographed sample (figure 11-6b) is outlined with gold cord; wings are gold with red circles, and butterfly has a blue body and antennae.

evaluation

Placement of decorative cord; glittering; neatness; and use of colors.

Photo Ornament

—students are delighted to see their photographs displayed on the class tree!

materials

- 1 sheet of construction paper
- scissors
- pencil
- tracing paper (optional)
- glitter
- 'white glue
- Christmas ornament hanger
- cellophane tape
- decorative cord
- school photograph (wallet size)
- paper punch

Draw construction paper ornament pattern. (See figure 11-7a.) See page 28 for enlarging technique. Cut out ornament along all solid lines.

Lay cut paper on flat surface, right side up. Run a bead of glue around photograph opening, and sprinkle with glitter. Glitter top of ornament and wherever else desired. Let glue dry.

Turn ornament over. Center photograph, face side down, over cut-out in ornament front. Tape in place. Now, 1 at a time, fold back 3 tabs on top of ornament. Secure with tape. Fold under bottom 4 tabs to complete ornament. Secure with tape.

Punch a hole in top center of ornament with a paper punch. Insert an 8"-long decorative cord in hole, and tie ends securely. Attach ornament to tree with a hanger. (See figure 11-7b.)

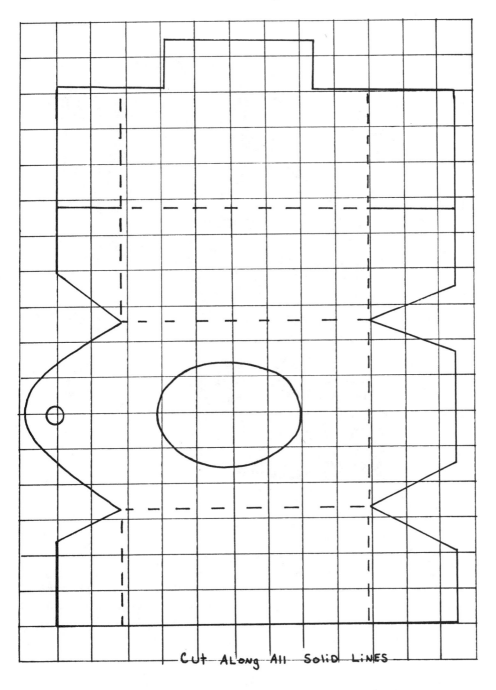

figure 11-7a *Pattern for Photo Ornament*

figure 11-7b   *Photo Ornament*

teaching tips

Decorate the class tree with these happy-faced ornaments. Everyone will enjoy his or her photograph hanging up for all to see.

Students can tape drawn pictures or cut-out designs from used Christmas cards inside the ornament opening. They can cut openings in each side of the ornament, too.

evaluation

Decoration; assembly of ornament; and completed ornament.

Cotton Ball Wreath

—a lovely idea for a Christmas package or your own front door!

materials

- 9 cotton balls (The cosmetic kind works nicely.)
- plastic foam meat tray (or heavy cardboard)
- glue
- 11 small red beads (or buttons)
- green and red felt scraps (optional)
- satin ribbon (optional)
- scissors
- florist wire
- tracing paper (optional)
- pencil
- artificial holly leaves (optional)
- tapestry needle
- Christmas ornament hanger

Make and cut out a cardboard wreath pattern. (See figure 11-8a.) Refer to page 28 for enlarging directions. Lay pattern on meat tray, trace and cut out. Use needle to punch 1 hole in top of wreath. Insert florist wire, and twist ends together to form hanging loop.

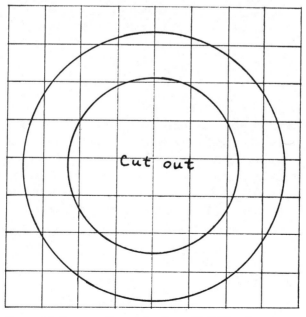

figure 11-8a   *Pattern for Cotton Ball Wreath*

Then glue 9 cotton balls on wreath form 1 at a time. Glue a small, red bead (or button) between every cotton ball. Let glue dry. Glue holly leaves on 1 cotton ball. Slip a hanger on florist wire to place ornament on tree. (See figure 11-8b.)

figure 11-8b   *Cotton Ball Wreath*

teaching tips

Students can cut holly leaves from green felt and make red felt berries with a paper punch. A pretty satin ribbon bow can also be tied on the wreath.

Small wreaths make fancy decorations for a Christmas package.

And, they can also be enlarged to create a lovely door wreath. Cut a larger wreath form from the side of a cardboard box. Cover cardboard form with aluminum foil (or paint a bright color), and glue several rows of cotton balls around wreath form. Decorate with small glass Christmas balls or lots of gingham bows. Wreaths can also be decorated with miniature pine cones and acorns. Attach florist wire through form to make a hanger.

evaluation

Neatness; placement of cotton balls; decoration; and originality.

Never-Melt Snowman

—egg cartons and cotton become a year-round, frosty friend!

materials

- bottom of a plastic egg carton
- white glue
- 4 cotton balls
- black construction paper
- scissors
- paper clip

figure 11-9a   *Never-Melt Snowman (left) originates from three cut-out sections of an egg carton (right). Glue cotton ball on protruding side of sections.*

Cut out 3 sections from an egg carton, and trim uneven edges with scissors. (See figure 11-9a.)

Stretch and fluff cotton balls. Egg sections protruding upward, glue cotton balls on all 3 egg sections. Cut a hat, broom, eyes, nose and mouth from black construction paper. Glue all pieces in place.

Unfold a paper clip. Then punch a hole in top of snowman with paper clip, and insert small end into hole. Use large end to hang snowman on tree. (See figure 11-9b.)

figure 11-9b   *Never-Melt Snowman*

teaching tips

Pre-cut sections for kindergarten through second-grade students. Make other ornaments from egg cartons. (See page 138 for ideas. Eliminate finger hole from puppet directions.) Students can cut out 2 alike sections and glue them together back to back. Decorate both sides of protruding egg sections for a 2-sided ornament.

evaluation

Cutting of sections; originality; neatness; and visual appeal of completed ornament.

chapter twelve —

Make It Together

No one person can do everything alone. Society thrives on communication and cooperation. Group activities stress and develop individual educational, physical, social and emotional values.

Through group activities students work, learn, laugh, play, share, enjoy and communicate with each other. "Look what we did!" group projects give all students a feeling of worthiness, responsibility, self-importance, reliability and a sense of belonging.

Many of the ideas in this chapter can be expanded to include the entire student body, benefiting both the students and the school. By becoming more aware of their physical surroundings and each other, students will feel needed and will cultivate new friendships through learning and playing.

The educational values in this chapter are all-encompassing. Make It Together and see!

Door Book Review

—show what you know on the door!

materials

- an existing door
- wrapping paper, art paper or newsprint (enough to cover an average-sized door)
- enamel or water base paint (optional)
- paint brushes (optional)
- various colors of poster board (or construction paper)

- scissors
- pencil
- thumbtacks (optional)
- ruler
- a book (fiction or nonfiction)
- paper and cellophane tape
- glue (or paste)
- liquid or dry tempera paint (optional)
- school paper (1 sheet per student)

First, you or your students should select a book to review. Tie it in with a lesson you are studying to stimulate interest and learning.

Read the book, and ask each student to submit a sketch describing how he or she would like to see book reviewed on the door. Select best sketch or combine several sketches. Draft a new sketch, as close to scale as possible, for a working guideline.

Assemble materials required to make door book review. Assign students, or let them volunteer, to work on a certain phase of book review.

Prepare background of door, and cover it with wrapping paper, newspaper, newsprint or art paper. Then thumbtack or tape covering on door, or, paint it any color desired.

Draw light pencil (or chalk) lines on door indicating where any words, letters, or illustrations should be placed. Students can paint letters and words directly on door or cut them out of construction paper (or poster board).

Decorate door with pictures, illustrations or items that pertain to subject of book being reviewed.

Students can draw, paint or cut out magazine pictures and glue (or tape) them on door. (See figure 12-1.)

teaching tips

A door book review is a great classroom project, or it can also be a competitive intra-school project.

Classes can select their own book to review, or books can be assigned by a judging committee. Appoint a committee of 3 or 5 unbiased judges (such as parents, artists, librarians or members of the news media). The judges can present merit awards to the classes who designed and constructed the best overall book review; the most original; the most colorful; the most humorous; the most graphic, etc.

Each class should participate. Students should be given an opportunity to see each decorated door. The project will stimulate an interest in books and encourage reading, while providing a wholesome competitiveness among students. It gives

figure 12-1   *Door Book Review*

students an opportunity to express originality and imagination, while at the same time, it makes them eager to know the contents of the book being reviewed.

Keep designs simple and free of clutter. The decorated door should provide each student with an immediate, visual idea of the contents of the reviewed book.

evaluation

Selection of book; neatness; thought content; originality; balance; design; use of color; perspective; resemblance of book review to subject of book reviewed; and completed project.

Springy Tire Garden

—neat, easy way to grow vegetables and flowers!

materials

- old rubber tire (or tires)
- garden tools (shovel, rake, hoe, etc.)
- vegetable or flower seeds (or plants)
- fertilizer (optional)
- bucket (or garden hose for watering)
- water
- empty coffee can with lid
- top soil (optional)
- permanent marking pen
- wooden paint stirrer (1 for each tire garden)

Select a site for the garden, considering growing conditions required for kinds of seeds (or plants) you intend to grow (sunny, partial shade, warm, etc.).

Requirements, recommended planting dates and germination periods are listed on backs of most seed packages.

Place tire on site. Students working in groups of 3 or 4 can set tire aside to prepare soil. Break up ground with a shovel (or hoe); then rake ground smooth. Set tire back over prepared soil, and plant seeds (or plants). Follow seed package planting directions.

Identify each tire garden by writing name of plant and a code number of group who is tending tire garden on a wooden paint stirrer. Stick stirrer inside tire garden, or you can identify garden by painting information on tire with white paint.

Water plants when necessary, according to package directions. Store original seed packages and leftover seeds in a coffee can so students can refer to growing directions. (See figure 12-2.)

figure 12-2   *Springy Tire Garden*

teaching tips

If the soil is poor you may need to add top soil to garden site before planting. Or, fertilize growing plants according to package recommendations.

All students like to watch things grow. School gardens are exciting. The rubber tire garden requires little care and is protected from being stepped upon. The tire makes the job of watering, weeding and cultivating easier.

A good educational project, gardens can be coordinated with a lesson on nature, science or the study of plants.

Students will be anxious to know all about how to care for their garden and will eagerly watch it grow.

Students can utilize the tire protection system when planting saplings or small flowering bushes on the school campus. Tie the planting of trees in with Arbor Day or ecology week activities.

Check with a local garden club, nursery or individuals to find sources for free saplings, plants or seeds.

Students in each work group can share gardening responsibilities of watering, weeding and cultivating.

If your climate has a short growing season, begin flower or vegetable plants inside the classroom. Cut several gallon plastic jugs in half, and fill almost full with rich dirt. Plant seeds, taking care not to overcrowd the container. Cover planted container with clear plastic wrap after you have watered well. Place container in sunlight. When the seeds sprout, remove plastic wrap. Continue growing plants inside until weather permits transplanting outdoors. (See package directions for a time schedule. Usually indoor planting can begin 3 or 4 weeks in advance of outdoor planting.)

Students should take care not to disturb root systems during transplanting.

Some easy-to-grow vegetables are carrots, corn, beans, cucumbers, squash and tomatoes.

If you have no access to campus ground for a garden site, students can plant flower gardens in the classroom. Old wash tubs, plastic and clay flower pots and paper milk cartons, even plastic egg cartons make good containers.

Follow seed package directions for growing requirements. Some annuals that are easy to grow indoors are coleus, cornflowers, marigolds and zinnias.

Students can also grow spices and herbs such as dill, parsely, chives and sage.

evaluation

Soil preparation; success of planted seeds (or plants); and students' care of garden.

Patchwork Spool Table

—fancy table for work or play!

materials

- 1 wooden cable spool (from a telephone or utility company)
- sandpaper (optional)
- enamel paint (spray or can)
- paint brush (optional)
- interior water base paint (optional)
- assorted colors of carpet remnants
- assorted colors of yarn scraps
- white glue
- scissors
- carpet cutting tool (or comparable substitute)
- water (optional)
- old newspapers
- old rags
- old (or protective) clothing

Turn carpet face down. (It's easier to cut backing of carpet.) Pre-cut carpet remnants into desired shapes and sizes for all students before beginning activity since carpet cutting tool is very sharp and too dangerous for elementary students to handle. While scissors may cut carpet, it is easier and quicker to use carpet cutting tool. Ask other teachers or aides to help cut carpet shapes. Store cut carpet shapes in a box until ready for use.

Cover a well-ventilated work area with newspapers, and place spool on newspaper. Clean spool (if necessary) with damp rags, and dry thoroughly.

Spray paint spool (or brush coat) with any color of enamel paint. (If possible, paint spool outside. Young students can paint their spool with washable interior paint for easy clean-up.) Let paint dry.

Place dry, painted spool on clean newspaper. (If outside, move spool into classroom.)

Now, unpack cut carpet shapes. The number of carpet shapes required will depend upon circumference of spool. (It took 55 rectangular carpet shapes to cover sample spool photographed, figure 12-3.)

Create basic patchwork design on a flat surface, alternating colors for a visual effect. To aid younger students, make a pattern out of newspaper the circumference of spool top. Lay paper pattern on floor, placing carpet squares in order on newspaper pattern.

When design is complete, coat top of spool with glue. Press cut carpet shapes

figure 12-3   *Patchwork Spool Table*

artwork courtesy of Frances Snyder

into place, beginning on outside edge and working toward center of spool. Space shapes evenly.

Continue placing carpet shapes until top of spool is covered. (If the glue dries, simply reapply.) Trim edges of carpet shapes where necessary to fit closer as you approach center of spool. Then fill in open spaces between carpet shapes with yarn glued in place. (See figure 12-3.)

teaching tips

The spool table can be made in stages: cleaning and sanding; painting; and gluing on carpet shapes.

The bottom and support post of spool can be covered with carpet shapes, too. If so, you need only paint outside rims of spool top and bottom.

Try to get spools in good condition. Those left outside for a long time will need some repair work before they can be painted. Wash spool, then sandpaper smooth before painting. Some spools have tops consisting of several boards while others have solid plywood tops. Plywood is preferable.

Students can make more than 1 spool table. Divide them into work groups, and see which group can produce the most effective patchwork design.

The spool has many uses. It can be used as a play center for young students, a comfortable sit-upon table for reading or it can be used to display handicrafts in the classroom or at an art show.

The spools come in various sizes. Smaller ones make ideal chairs and mini-display tables.

evaluation

Spool preparation; painting; carpet coverage; use of colors; originality; design; and completed project.

Pictorial Wall Mural

—walls painted beautifully!

materials

- an existing wall
- various colors of enamel paint
- various sizes of paint brushes
- old rags
- old newspapers
- chalk
- paper (for sketching)
- pencil

Select a plain, unadorned wall inside or outside classroom. Then, decide on central theme (or topic) of your pictorial.

Working as a group, students should sketch figures and characters, noting colors, background, tools or buildings, on paper.

If pictorial is historical in nature, utilize textbooks and specialized subject books to research characters involved, their costumes, colors, setting and dates of period. Make facts as accurate as possible.

Assemble sketches of proposed wall figures and characters, and mark their proper placement on wall with chalk. Take care to properly balance pictorial on wall, and keep figures in perspective.

Now, older or more artistic students can draw characters and figures on wall with chalk, where indicated. (For young students, you can draw figures or ask a local artist to sketch basic figures for you.)

After all characters and figures have been sketched with chalk, cover work area floor with newspapers. Using a small brush, outline each chalk line with black enamel paint. Let paint dry. (The local artist might also outline figures and characters for you.)

When black paint dries, denote, with chalk, the color of paint for each figure or character inside area outlined in black. Lay it out like a paint-by-number picture.

Students can paint inside areas according to color denoted. Paint all pictures. (See figure 12-4a.)

figure 12-4a   *Pictorial Wall Mural*

artwork courtesy of Frances Smith

When paint is dry, correct any mistakes with black enamel along outlines or touch-up with original wall paint. Let paint dry. (See figure 12-4b.) Wipe off any chalk lines with a soft cloth.

teaching tips

Keep sample sketches until mural is complete. Then if chalk lines are accidentally erased, questions can easily be answered by referring to original sketches.

If basic wall to be painted is dirty or the color is not appropriate, paint wall before beginning the activity. Save some paint for later touch-ups.

figure 12-4b   *Paint black finishing details on each picture, such as whiskers, buttons, eyelashes, plaids, etc., for a professional-looking pictorial wall mural.*

artwork courtesy of Frances Smith

The sample photographs depict a pictorial time line of America's first 200 years. The mural is divided into 2 sections: the first 100 years features pilgrims, patriotism and pioneers; the second 100 years pictures electricity, mechanization and space exploration.

The exterior wall used is divided in center by the Great Seal of the United States. The 200 years are tied together with a continuously flowing red, white and blue ribbon.

Utilize various sizes of brushes during painting. Use small brushes to outline, fill in small areas and touch-up. Use large brushes for background and large areas.

Enamel paint is recommended for interior and exterior murals. It is waterproof, dries fast and boasts vivid colors.

Bear in mind that a little paint goes a long way. Ask a local merchant, individual or paint store to donate supplies or their cost. (It's surprisingly nominal.) Students can bring leftover paint and old brushes from home.

Enamel paint does drip a little, so keep a wipe up cloth handy.

The pictorial mural can be a vivid teaching tool. You or your students can write a brief paragraph about the figures or period of pictorial. Mimeograph this composition and distribute it to students and guests to better acquaint them with the pictorial.

Students will not only learn about their painted subjects, but will also retain this knowledge since the pictorial will be a constant reminder.

A class project can easily turn into a school project. Each class can be assigned a wall space and complete their portion of pictorial. A mural of such proportions requires a well-researched, drawn-out master plan. A student/teacher committee can be placed in charge of the production.

In addition to learning by doing, students will be beautifying their school. They will be proud and protective of their artwork.

Wall murals and figures can be painted strictly for decoration, too. Individual cartoon characters and figures such as barnyard animals, old-fashioned trains, comical insects and pop art items can be painted on classroom, restroom, library or cafeteria walls.

With care, the pictorial will last for years. If the background requires repainting, simply paint around each figure or character. It takes a little more time, but the highly prized pictorial will be preserved.

evaluation

Theme of pictorial; appropriateness of figures and characters to theme; accuracy of historical facts and details; painting; neatness; and completed project.

Holey Sculpture

—balloons and plaster make unique sculptures!

materials

- plaster of Paris (approximately 7 cups per carton)
- ½ gallon paper milk carton (washed and dried)
- 4 or 5 small balloons
- measuring cup
- water
- old newspapers
- scissors
- plastic dish pan (or container to mix plaster in)
- coarse and fine sandpaper
- metal teaspoon (optional)
- kitchen paring knife (optional)
- ceramic cleaning tool

- wood stain, tempera paint or felt-tipped pens (optional)
- paint brushes (optional)

Cover work area with old newspapers. (This is a dandy outdoor activity.)

Use scissors to cut off top portion of milk carton. (Cut carton will stand approximately 7½″ high.) Then 1 at a time, fill 2 or 3 balloons ½ full with water. (Slip neck of balloon over faucet to fill.) Knot neck of balloon (or tie tightly with string).

Fill 1 or 2 balloons halfway with air. Lay air-filled balloons in bottom of carton. Then, lay water-filled balloons on top.

Mix plaster of Paris in a dish pan according to package directions. (It takes approximately 7 cups of plaster and 3½ cups of water to fill 1 carton.)

Pour mixed plaster into carton. (Don't worry about top balloons protruding out of plaster.) Set carton aside until plaster sets up. (It takes approximately 30 minutes to 1 hour, depending upon brand of plaster used.)

When plaster is hard, tear away carton. It is easiest to start at top and tear down toward base. Hold plaster form over a sink (or pail) and pop balloons with scissor points (or a sharp pencil). Let water drain from plaster, and pull out broken balloon pieces from plaster.

Place holey sculpture on dry newspaper. Remove rough edges created by balloons, and smooth with a paring knife, spoon edge or ceramic cleaning tool. (It's best to work with freshly poured plaster since it is still rather soft and can be carved and smoothed more easily.)

Sandpaper remaining rough edges smooth. Leave holey sculpture as it is or paint with tempera, felt-tipped pens or stain. Insert a small altar candle inside a hole in the sculpture for a unique effect. (See figure 12-5.)

teaching tips

This activity is easy for fourth-, fifth- and sixth-grade students. They will need some supervision, especially when handling carving tools.

Younger students will need help tying knots in their balloons. Mix plaster for them to prevent waste, and make sure plaster is properly prepared. They can safely use a ceramic cleaning tool (with proper supervision) to carve their sculpture; but for ultimate safety, limit them to a teaspoon and sandpaper.

You can make smaller sculptures by using 1-pint and 1-quart paper milk cartons instead of the ½-gallon size.

evaluation

Basic design of completed sculpture; imagination; originality; painting (if any); and visual effect of completed sculpture.

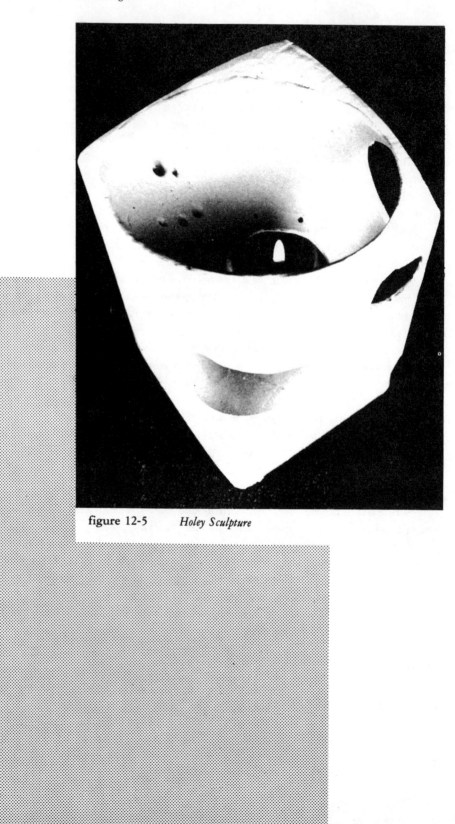

figure 12-5   *Holey Sculpture*

appendix —

Where-to-Find-It Craft Supply List

places

- art supply stores

- beauty parlors

- business offices

- dress makers, upholsterers, fabric mills, drapery companies
- florists

- friends and neighbors

- furniture and appliance stores

things

- dried-up tempera paint (much of which can be made good again with water), faded or bent poster board
- panty hose plastic eggs, used fingernail polish
- old pencils, magazines, paper scraps, old stamp pads, old felt-tipped pens
- material scraps, thin tissue paper

- dried flowers, faded artificial flowers, ribbon scraps, ferns and leaves
- yarn scraps, greeting cards, old jewelry, cereal boxes, comic pages, detergent bottles, glass jars, nail polish, butter and margarine containers, soda can rings, milk cartons, scraps of lace, rick-rack, decorative trim
- cardboard boxes

- grocery stores
- cardboard boxes, grocery bags, old vegetables, berry baskets, spilled or outdated items like macaroni, flour and salt

- hotels and motels
- soap, paper towels rolls

- landscaping companies
- rocks, tiny plants, silica sand

- laundries, laundromats and dry cleaners
- plastic gallon and half-gallon jugs, detergent bottles, detergent boxes, coat hangers

- lumber yards and carpentry shops
- wood scraps

- newspapers, printers, publishing companies
- paper scraps

- nurseries and day-care centers
- baby food jars, old coloring books and children's books

- nursing homes
- pill bottles, greeting and Christmas cards

- paint stores
- wooden paint stirrers, leftover paint

- restaurants and cafeterias
- egg cartons, aluminum pie pans, frozen juice cans, tin cans, plastic cups, glass jars, old potatoes, half-pint milk cartons

- tile manufacturers, tile setters, builders
- leftover, mismatched and broken tile, silica sand

- variety and drug stores
- broken beads, damaged goods, material, old nail polish

Index